FUN CRAFTS FOR KIDS

FUN
CRAFTS
FOR
KIDS

Jann Haworth
Joan Jones
Irene Newington
and
Clare Beaton

MEREHURST

Contents

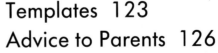

Paint

To begin painting all that you need is a bit of space, some paint, a few basic tools, and lots of imagination. Some of the tools that you might find useful are pictured here. Turn the page for advice on paintbrushes, as well as some other ideas for putting paint on paper. And remember there is no right way to paint. Do not worry if your pictures don't look anything like the ones in this book — that's all part of the fun

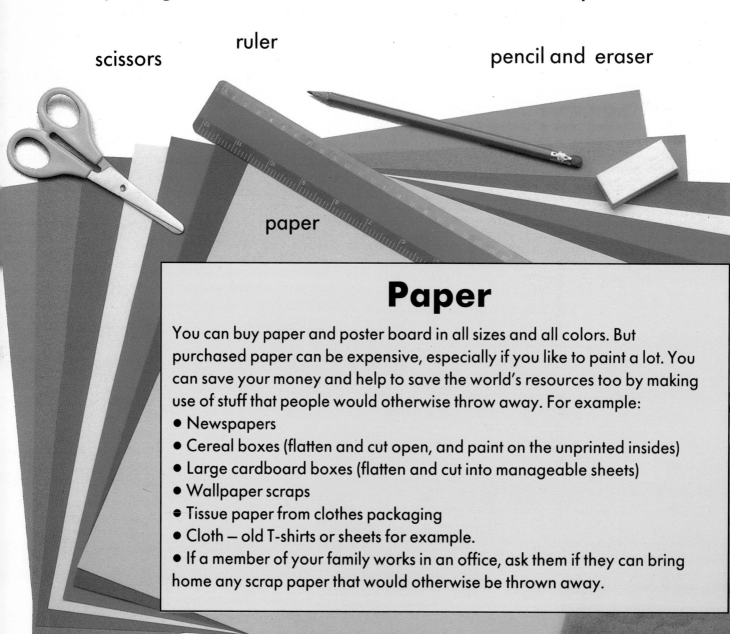

scissors

ruler

pencil and eraser

paper

Paper

You can buy paper and poster board in all sizes and all colors. But purchased paper can be expensive, especially if you like to paint a lot. You can save your money and help to save the world's resources too by making use of stuff that people would otherwise throw away. For example:
- Newspapers
- Cereal boxes (flatten and cut open, and paint on the unprinted insides)
- Large cardboard boxes (flatten and cut into manageable sheets)
- Wallpaper scraps
- Tissue paper from clothes packaging
- Cloth — old T-shirts or sheets for example.
- If a member of your family works in an office, ask them if they can bring home any scrap paper that would otherwise be thrown away.

Paints

Water-based paints have been used for all the projects in this book. You can buy them ready-mixed in large, easy-to-use, squeeze bottles. The basic colors you will need are red, yellow, blue, black and white. From these you can mix all other colors, as you will see on page 10. You can use acrylic paints which come in tubes, but do avoid powder paints: they are dusty, difficult to make up and the colors do not mix well. You can add water to paint to make it thinner or white glue to make it thicker.

metal ruler

poster board

string

craft knife

masking tape

white glue

felt-tip pens

water-based paint

acrylic paint

wax crayons

oil-based crayons

tissue paper

Remember

☆ Wear an apron and cover the work area.
☆ Always ask an adult for help when you see this sign [!]
☆ Clean up after yourself.

7

Brush Up On Painting

When you begin to paint, you will need to paint with something. The first thing you might think of is a paint-brush, but there are lots of other things you could use. Blow puddles of thin paint around with a straw. Use your fingers, hands or cut vegetables to print with. Make a cardboard comb and twist it through thick paint, or dabble and smear paint on with a rag. Draw with a twig dipped in thin paint. Last but not least, look at all the different kinds of brushes you could use and try them out for yourself.

plastic comb

plastic straws

twig

cardboard comb

roller

cut potato

hands

newspaper

Useful Things to Collect

All sorts of things around the home can be used to print paint onto paper. Why not make a collection. Here are some ideas to start you off:

Corrugated cardboard, bubble pack, corks, cotton spools, sponges, fiberfill, jars with the labels still on, leaves, cut fruit and vegetables, pieces of wood, cloth, old shoes, boxes, etc.

cloths

decorating brushes

paintbrushes

toothbrush

nailbrush

scrubbing brush

shaving brush

9

Color Mixing

What color will it make? All you will need is a basic set of paints (see page 7), a white plate and a brush to find out!

Mix red and yellow to make orange. Add more red for a warmer orange and more yellow for a tangerine shade.

Blue and yellow mixed together make green. You can vary the shade by adding more or less yellow or blue.

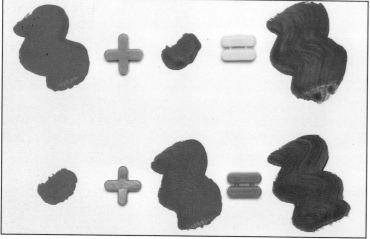

Mix a brushful of red with a drop of blue. Now try a drop of red with a brushful of blue. How is it different?

Red and green mixed together make brown. Now try orange and blue.

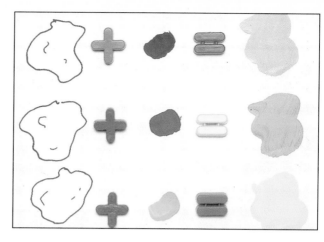

To make pastel colors, simply add a drop of any colored paint to white paint.

Now see what happens when you mix a drop of black to any color.

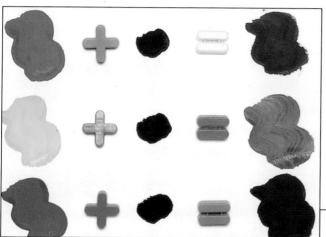

Skin tones are harder to mix. Here are a couple of examples. Now try to mix a color to match your skin.

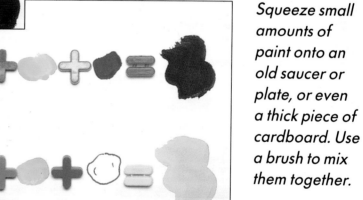

Squeeze small amounts of paint onto an old saucer or plate, or even a thick piece of cardboard. Use a brush to mix them together.

What an Effect

Try using some of the tools on pages 8 and 9 to explore these painting techniques.

Dry brush

Put a little paint onto the tip of a dry brush and work it into the bristles by brushing lightly on newspaper. Now paint onto paper — try adding other colors.

Stippling

Cut out a shape from paper and place onto poster board. Dab around the edges of the cut-out shape with a lightly-painted brush.

Rolling and combing

1 Roll a thick layer of paint onto a sheet of poster board. If you do not have a roller, use a jar with the label still on it.

2 Make a comb by cutting teeth along one edge of a square of thick cardboard. Drag and twist the comb through the paint.

Splattering

Dip a toothbrush into some watered-down paint. Run a paintbrush handle along its bristles to splatter the paint onto the paper. What effect will you get with a nailbrush?

Newspaper crumple

Crumple a piece of newspaper into a crumpled ball. Dab into paint and print onto paper. Use other balls of crumpled paper to add more colors.

IN THE FRAME
Frame your pictures as you paint them. Cut 2 L-shaped pieces of thick cardboard. Position these onto the paper so that they mark off a rectangular angle. Paint within this area and then remove the cardboard pieces for an instant frame.

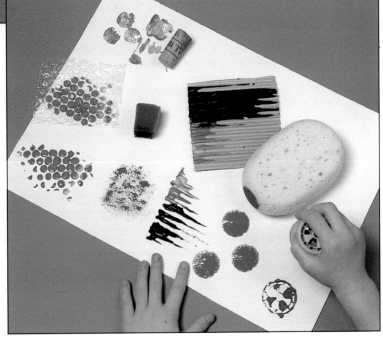

You can use all sorts of things collected from around the house to paint with. Now see what you can find.

13

The Background Story

Why use only plain paper to draw or paint on when you can create an interesting textured background?

Streaking and dripping

Dip a middle-sized decorating brush into watered-down paint and hold the brush at the top of the paper. Lift the paper and let the paint drip down.

Washes

Dip a large decorating brush into watered-down paint and brush across the paper. Now add different colored washes, letting the colors run into each other.

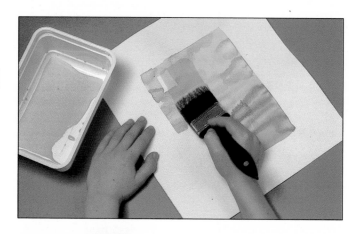

Muting

1 Paint thickly onto a sheet of paper. Cover an area of the painted paper with newspaper and flatten with your hand.

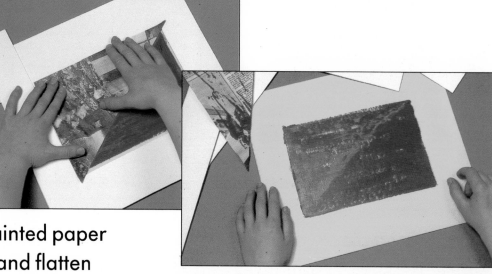

2 Carefully lift off the newspaper.

14

Rag rolling

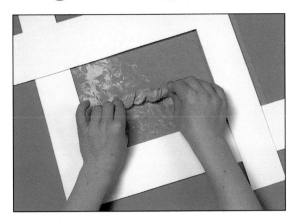

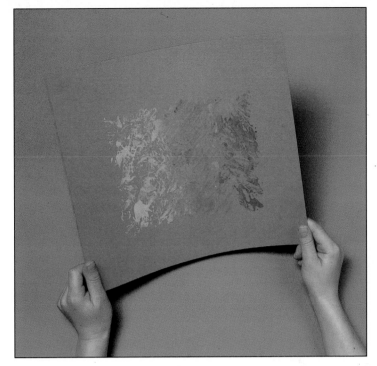

1 Put a rag into a tray of paint and stir until it is well covered. Gather into a wrinkled sausage. Place at the bottom left-hand corner of the paper and roll up.

2 Continue to roll the rag in columns across the paper. If the rag print becomes faint, dip the rag in paint again.

Staining

!1 You can use all sorts of household products to stain white paper, for example shoe polish, turmeric, vinegar, coffee, food coloring and soy sauce. Make up a sample sheet like the one in the photograph.

2 Choose your favorite one and stain some sheets of white paper for future paintings. This tea wash is used as a background for the next project in this book.

Me! Me! Me!

A good place to start painting is with a portrait of yourself.

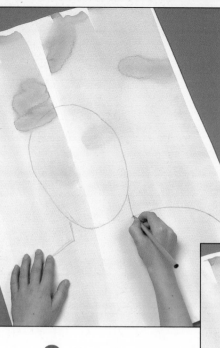

1 Take a textured sheet of paper. Sit in front of a mirror and look at the shape of your face. Draw the outline of it in the center of the paper.

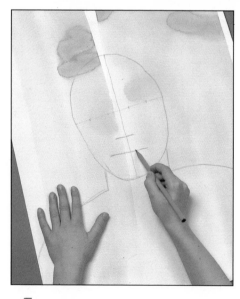

2 Divide the face up into quarters by marking in light pencil lines horizontally and vertically.

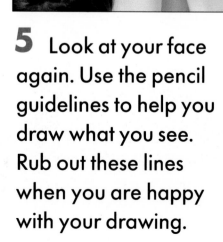

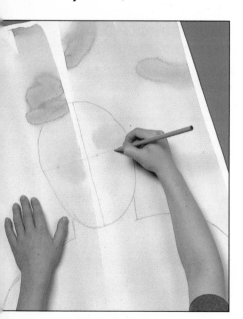

3 Divide the horizontal or eyeline into fifths, to give you a guide for positioning the corners of the eyes.

4 Mark in lines for the nose and mouth on the bottom half of the vertical line.

5 Look at your face again. Use the pencil guidelines to help you draw what you see. Rub out these lines when you are happy with your drawing.

6 Before beginning to paint over your drawing make a copy of it. Tape it onto a window and place a sheet of paper on top of it. Trace your drawing.

7 Paint over your original drawing. Try to match the color of your eyes and hair. Mark in any freckles. Don't forget your eyebrows and eyelashes.

Trace copies from your original to make countless versions of yourself.

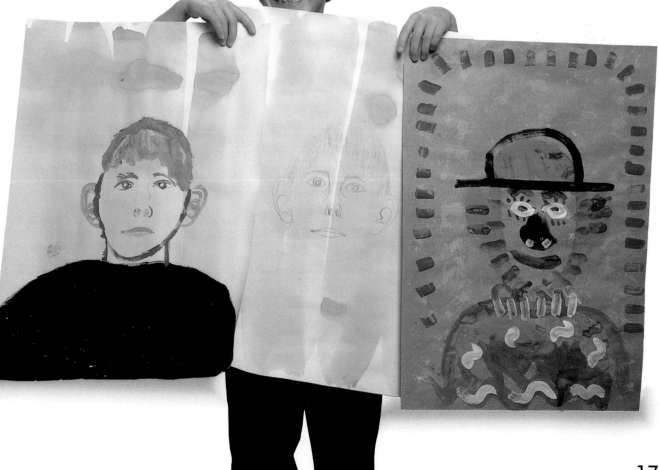

Fruit and Vegetable Printing

Instead of painting a still life of a bowl of fruit, use the fruit (and some vegetables too) to paint the picture!

!1 Ask your mom or dad if you can have a selection of fruit and vegetables to paint with.

!2 Now ask your parent if he or she could cut up the fruit and vegetables so that you can print with them.

3 Put out the colors you will need onto a plate. Paint the cut end of a vegetable and begin to print a border around a large sheet of paper.

4 The painted edge of a carrot stick has been used to print this bowl and the placemat beneath it.

5 An apple cut in half and painted has been used to print different colored apples in the bowl.

6 The round end of a carrot has been used to build up a bunch of grapes. A half a lemon has been used to print an orange. The round end of a carrot painted red makes the cherries.

You can have great fun experimenting with the variety of effects that can be achieved with this simple printing technique.

Tree of Life Stencil

A stencil is made by cutting a pattern from a piece of poster board or paper. It can then be painted over to reproduce the same pattern as many times as you like.

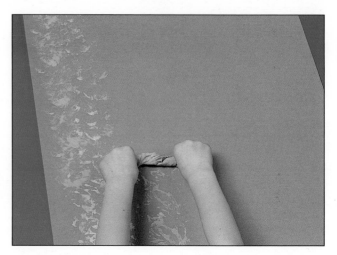

1 Rag roll over a sheet of paper using a slightly lighter shade of paint than the color of the paper. Leave to dry.

2 To make the trunk and branches of the tree, paint your hand and forearm brown and print at the bottom of the paper.

3 Draw half shapes of leaves, butterflies, hearts, flowers and stars along the folded line of some small squares of white paper. Cut out the shapes and open up the paper. These are your stencils.

4 Put a stencil on the ragged paper. Stipple the paint all over the stencil. Take care that the paint does not seep under the edge of the stencil.

5 Fill out the shape of the tree by painting a pattern of stencils across the paper. Leave to dry.

The finished picture. Now make several versions. Cut more stencils – try varying the shapes of the leaves.

6 To add some detail to your picture, cut a leaf vein stencil from paper. Place the stencil over the painted leaves and stipple with black paint.

Draw With Glue

A picture drawn with glue makes a wonderful printing block.

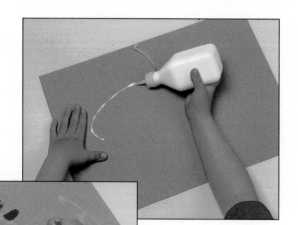

1 Use glue to draw a picture onto a piece of thick cardboard. Leave to dry overnight.

2 When the glue has dried completely, color in the areas between the lines with wax or oil-based crayons.

3 Paint all over the surface of the cardboard. Work fast so that the paint does not dry.

4 Lay a sheet of white tissue-paper over the painted cardboard and smooth down with your hands. Carefully peel back the tissue paper.

5 Put the tissue-paper print to one side to dry.

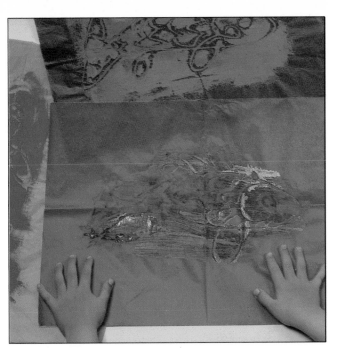

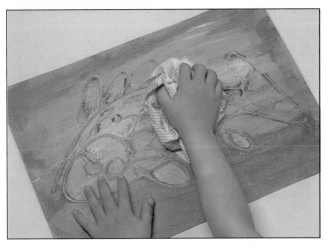

7 When you have made all the prints you want, use a damp cloth to wipe most of the paint off the cardboard. Leave some paint in the corners. When you have finished, the color of the crayons should be showing through brightly again.

6 Paint all over the cardboard again. This time make a print onto a colored sheet of tissue paper. You can make as many prints of your picture as you like.

The printing cardboard has become a picture in itself. Make a frame for it and hang it on the wall.

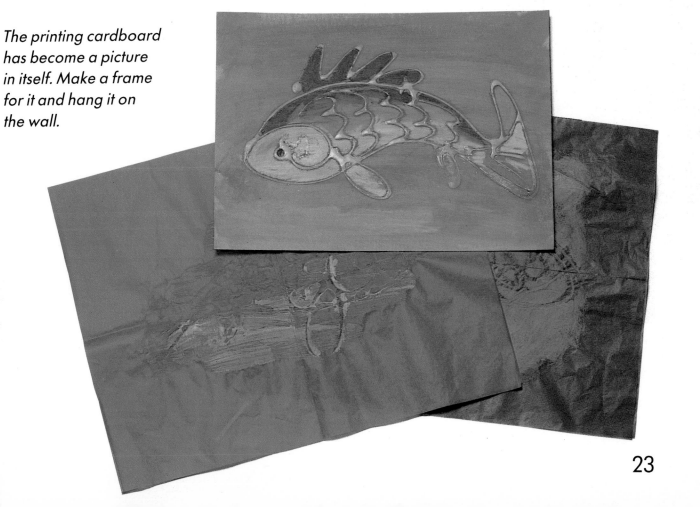

Cloth Printing

Transform an old sheet with a little paint and a simple printing block made from poster board.

Materials

newspapers

thick poster board

cloth

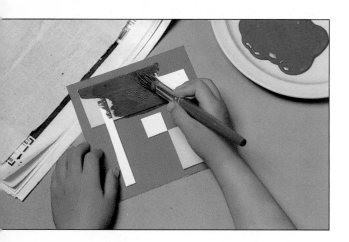

⚠ 1 Cut out shapes from thick poster board.

2 Arrange the cut shapes into a pattern on a square of thick poster board and glue in position. Make several printing blocks and leave to dry overnight.

⚠ 3 Cut out a 24" x 24" square of cloth, iron and place on a bed of newspaper (6–8 layers) ready for printing onto. Quickly apply a thick layer of paint to a printing block.

4 Press the block down hard on the bottom edge of the cloth. Print another square next to the first, and so on.

24

! 5 As the print fades, put more paint on the block. Paint a pyramid of printed squares. When the paint has dried, place the cloth upside down on the newspaper and iron.

! 6 Prepare another piece of cloth. Paint 2 printing blocks different colors and use in turn to print rows of squares.

7 To make placemats, cut out the printed squares. Make a fringe by pulling out the threads along the edges of the cloth.

Ask an adult to help you sew together 2 pieces of printed cloth to make a cushion cover.

FABRIC PAINTS
If you use ordinary paint for printing, the things you make from the printed cloth will not be washable. You can buy special fabric paints from an art store that can be washed. These are used in exactly the same way.

25

String Pictures

In this project you will use string to draw with, print with and to make a decorative frame.

Materials

shells

string

thick
poster board

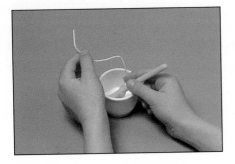

1 Put a long piece of string into a cupful of glue and stir it around.

2 Take the string out of the glue and pull it through your fingers so that it does not drip everywhere.

3 Lay the string on top of a small square of poster board ($4^3/_4$" x $4^3/_4$") to make a picture. You may need to cut the string into small pieces. Leave your string picture to dry overnight.

4 Lay paper onto a bed of newspaper. Paint over the string picture and press down hard onto the paper. Make several prints.

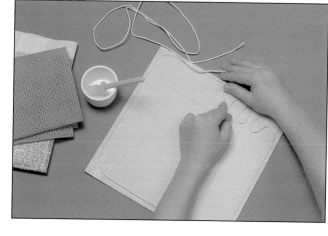

5 Choose your favorite print and frame it. Put the string picture in the center of a large square of poster board (6¾" x 6¾"), draw around it and lift it off.

6 Decorate the border by drawing on a pattern with glue-covered string. Stick on some shells. Leave overnight to dry.

7 Color in the spaces around the string and the shells with wax or oil-based crayons.

8 To give the frame an antique effect, paint the poster board brown. Use a rag to dab off some of the paint.

Cut a print down to fit into the center of the frame. Glue into place. Ask an adult to hang it up for you.

27

Painter's Sketchbook

Make this book to keep your favorite pictures in.

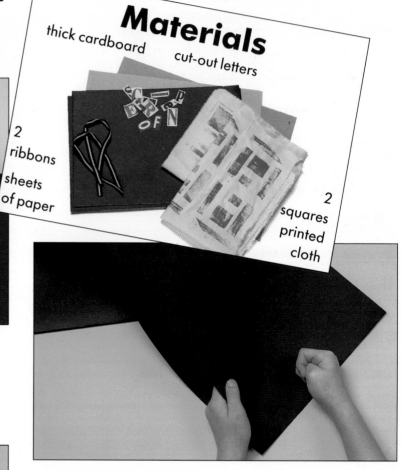

Materials
thick cardboard
cut-out letters
2 ribbons
sheets of paper
2 squares printed cloth

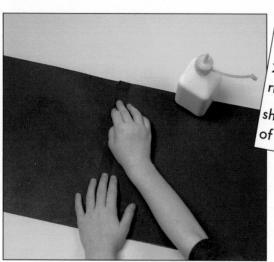

1 Make a long strip of paper by gluing several sheets of paper end to end.

2 Fold evenly into a zig zag.

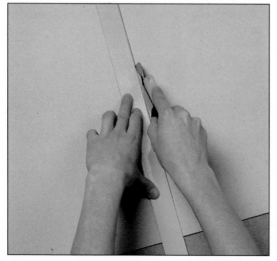

⚠ 3 Cut 2 pieces of thick cardboard about ½" larger all around than the folded zig zag of paper.

4 Now cover both pieces of cardboard with the printed cloth made on page 20. Place the cardboard on the cloth. Cut around the fabric leaving 1" edge.

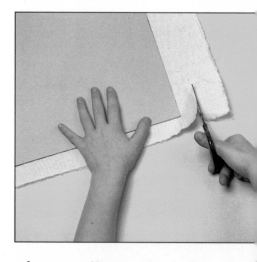

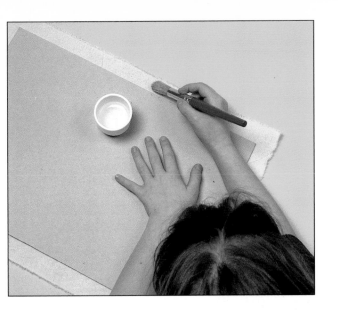

5 Use a brush to dampen the edges of the cloth with water.

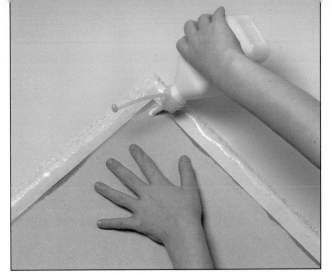

6 Run a line of glue all around the edge of the cloth and a blob on each corner of the cardboard.

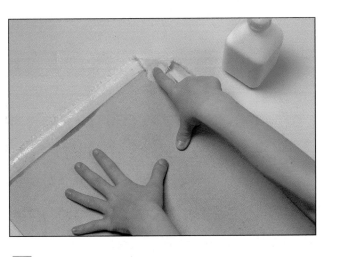

7 Fold the corners of the cloth over onto the cardboard as shown.

8 Fold over the sides of the cloth as shown. Make sure that the corner seams do not overlap each other, and check that the fabric is pulled tight across the front of the cardboard.

9 Glue a length of ribbon onto each piece of cardboard.

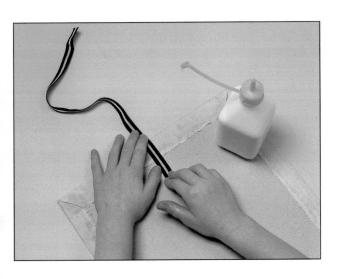

Continues on next page

10 Evenly spread a thin layer of glue over both pieces of cardboard.

11 Run a thin line of glue close to the edge of the first page of the zig zag strip of paper. Press the paper onto a piece of covered cardboard.

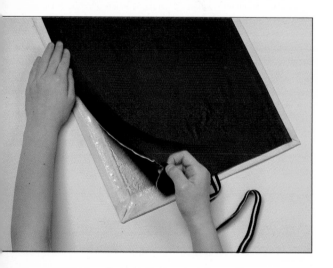

12 Glue around the last page of the zig zag strip and press onto the second piece of covered cardboard. Make sure that the ribbons are both on the same side so they can be tied together.

14 Cut out letters from magazine or newspaper headlines and make a title for your book.

13 Once the glue has dried (leave overnight) open up the accordion book and print a border around each page using a cut potato.

Fill your book with your favorite pictures painted by you, your family and your friends. When it is full, make a present of it to a friend.

31

Fresco

Paint a picture onto the plaster surface of a small sheet of plasterboard and hang it on the wall. Plasterboard is cheap and can be bought from any art store.

1 Use a large decorating brush to cover both sides of the plasterboard with water. Leave overnight to dry.

2 Draw a large rectangle on the front of the board leaving an even frame all around.

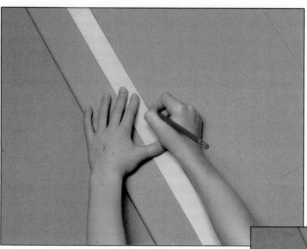

[!] 3 Ask an adult to cut through the paper along the marked lines just into the plaster below.

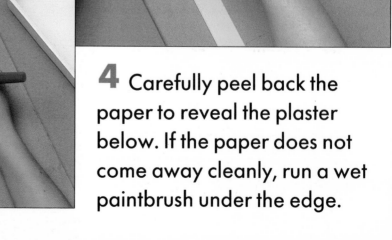

4 Carefully peel back the paper to reveal the plaster below. If the paper does not come away cleanly, run a wet paintbrush under the edge.

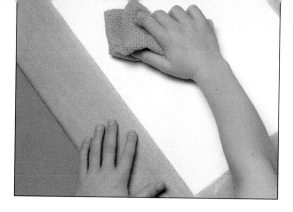

5 Scrub the plaster with a damp cloth. Scrap off any remaining patches of paper with a round-ended knife. Don't worry if the surface of the plaster looks scratched or pitted. This will give a more interesting effect when painted over.

6 Paint a picture onto the plaster using watered-down paints. Try a portrait of your mom or dad, or your pet.

7 Use stencils cut from thin poster board to decorate the paper frame. Use a thick brush to stipple the paint onto the stencil, taking care not to let paint seep under the edge.

Furniture Painting

An old piece of furniture can be transformed by your imagination and just a little paint. But do ask mom or dad for permission first.

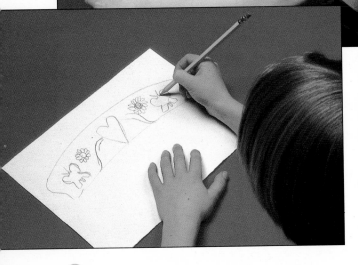

1 Use fine sandpaper to rub down the area of wood to be painted.

2 Put a little dishwashing liquid into a bowl of warm water and wash down the sanded wood. Leave to dry.

3 Sketch out a rough design for the area to be painted. This is just a guide, and you can change it as you work.

4 Cut all the stencils you will need from thin poster board.

5 Work out from the center of your design. Tape the stencil to the wood.

6 Use a thick brush to dab paint over the stencil.

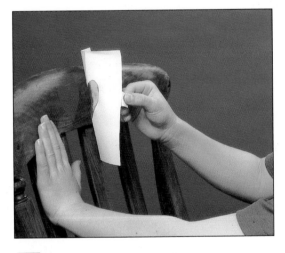

!7 Carefully peel off the stencil. Build up your design using one stencil at a time. Once the paint has dried ask an adult to help you brush the painted area with a thin coat of varnish.

The finished chair. Now everyone will want to sit on it.

Modeling

You can make models from all sorts of different materials including homemade play dough that can be used time and time again, and papier-mâché which is made from old newspapers and a flour and water paste. Before you begin to make your models it is a good idea to get ready some useful tools.

Kitchen Equipment

You will also need some standard kitchen tools including:

Measuring cup, mixing bowl, bucket, plastic bowl, measuring spoons, baking tray, waxed paper, plastic wrap, chopping board, oven mitts, plastic spatula, wooden spoon, saucepan

petroleum jelly

ruler

pencil and eraser

felt-tip pens

poster paints

brushes

36

Other Useful Things

To cut and mark dough and clay
Plastic bottle caps, pen caps, jar lids, spoon handles, fork prongs, paper clips, buttons, knitting needles, straws, pasta, cotton spools, garlic press, toothpicks

For plaster molds
Any empty plastic food containers: yogurt cartons, egg trays, candy box trays, etc.

To decorate your models
Fabric scraps, felt, pipe cleaners, glitter, straws, buttons, pasta, beads, seeds, sequins, ribbons, pinecones, dried leaves and flowers, tree bark, shells, pebbles

hole punch

varnish or gloss

glue spreader

child's rolling pin

white glue

cutters

modeling tool

scissors

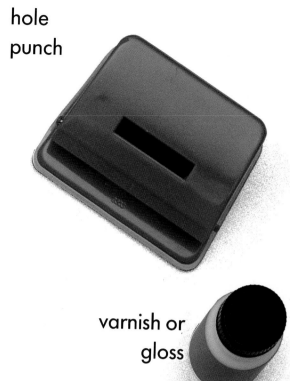

Remember

☆ Wear an apron and cover the work area
☆ Collect together the items in the materials box at the beginning of each project.
☆ Always ask an adult for help when you see this sign !
☆ Clean up after yourself.

Play Dough Fun

Play dough is quick and easy to make, but as it involves cooking you will need to ask a grown-up to help you.

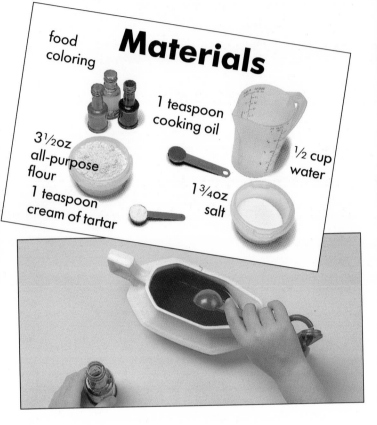

Materials

food coloring

1 teaspoon cooking oil

3½oz all-purpose flour

½ cup water

1 teaspoon cream of tartar

1¾oz salt

1 Put the flour, salt, cream of tartar and cooking oil into a saucepan and stir together.

2 Add 1–2 teaspoonfuls of red food coloring to the water and stir well. The more you add the deeper the color will be.

3 Gradually add the water to the other ingredients, mixing thoroughly to remove any lumps.

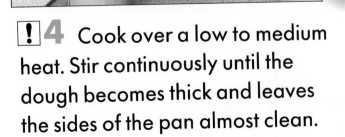

[!]4 Cook over a low to medium heat. Stir continuously until the dough becomes thick and leaves the sides of the pan almost clean.

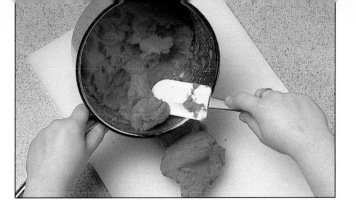

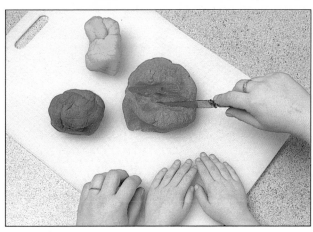

! **5** Scrape the mixture from the saucepan onto a smooth flat surface. Put the saucepan in to soak immediately. Make up two more batches of blue and yellow play dough.

! **6** Leave the play dough to cool for at least 10 minutes. Before using the dough ask an adult to cut through it with a knife to test that the inside has cooled too.

7 Knead the cooled play dough until it becomes smooth and pliable. You can mix the 3 colors to get a marbled effect.

8 You can make up a variety of colors by mixing together red, yellow and blue.
Red and yellow make orange.
Blue and yellow make green.
Red and blue make purple.

STORAGE TIP
Roll the play dough up into balls of the same color. Wrap each in plastic wrap and keep in an air-tight container in the refrigerator.

Play Dough Pictures

Roll out a ball of all the different colored play dough you have made.

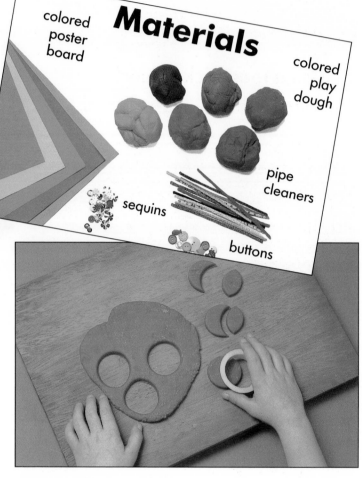

Materials

colored poster board

colored play dough

pipe cleaners

sequins

buttons

1 Cut out rectangles and squares from the rolled out play dough. Cut the squares in half to make triangles, and cut the triangles in half to make even smaller triangles.

2 Use bottle caps, jar lids and pastry cutters to cut out circles, ovals and crescent shapes.

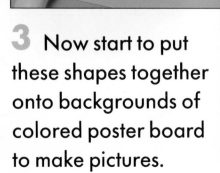

3 Now start to put these shapes together onto backgrounds of colored poster board to make pictures.

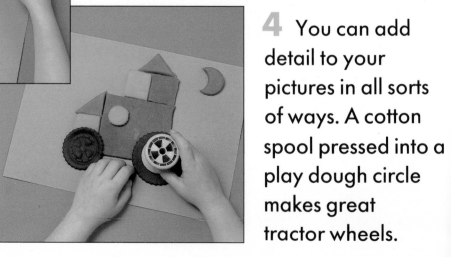

4 You can add detail to your pictures in all sorts of ways. A cotton spool pressed into a play dough circle makes great tractor wheels.

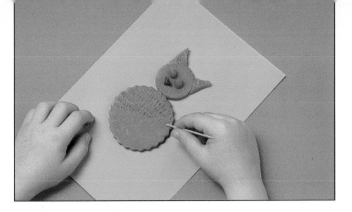

5 Use a toothpick to mark 'fur' onto a play dough animal.

You can have lots of fun adding the finishing touches to your picture.

6 A button bow tie and pipe cleaner whiskers finish off this cat *purr*fectly.

7 A paper clip can be used to mark on bird feathers or fish scales.

Play Dough Bakery

Remember, although these things look good enough to eat they wouldn't taste nice at all, so please don't try it!

Iced cherry cakes

1 Roll some small and large balls of the red play dough and some medium-sized balls of the yellow play dough.

Materials

colored play dough

plate

candy papers

2 Flatten a yellow ball between your fingers and drape over a large red ball. Top with a small red ball.

Croissants

3 Roll out some yellow play dough until it is very thin. Cut into squares.

4 Roll up a square from one corner. Bend into a crescent shape.

42

Jam tarts

5 Roll out some yellow play dough to about ¼" thick and cut out some circles with a small pastry cutter.

6 Press a small bottle cap in the center of each cut circle to make an indentation.

7 Place a ball of red or yellow play dough in the hollow and flatten to fill the space.

Why not try modeling a variety of fruits from your play dough, such as oranges, apples, cherries, grapes, bananas and pears. Use pipe cleaners to make stalks and leaves.

Salt Dough Medallions

Salt dough can be baked hard, painted and varnished so that you can keep the things you make forever.

Materials

ribbon

gold poster board

1 teaspoon cooking oil

1/3 cup water

3 1/2 oz all-purpose flour

1 3/4 oz salt

1 Mix together the salt, flour and cooking oil in a bowl. Add the water a little at a time and mix to a smooth paste that leaves the side of the bowl clean.

2 Place the dough onto a lightly floured board. Use a lightly floured rolling pin to roll out the dough to about 1/4" thick.

3 Use pastry cutters to cut out several shapes from the salt dough.

4 Use a paper clip to print a pattern on the medallions.

44

⚠ 5 Open the paper clip and prick out a circular pattern on the medallions. Place them onto a greased baking sheet and bake in a preheated oven at 250°F until they are firm (about 2 hours).

⚠ 6 Remove the medallions from the oven and leave to cool. Paint and lightly varnish. Decorate the medallions. To make a winning medal, cut a star from gold poster board and glue onto the center of one of the medallions.

7 Overlap the ends of the ribbon and glue together. Stick the medallion firmly to the overlapped ends of the ribbon.

The medallions can easily be changed into pins by simply taping a safety pin to the back of the decorated shapes.

Materials

ribbon

salt dough

felt

fabric

2 pipe cleaners

Faces On the Door

Follow the instructions for making salt dough on page 44, then use it to model these fun faces to hang over your bedroom door.

1 Lightly flour your hands and a board. Knead the dough on the board until it is smooth. Break off a small piece and put to one side.

2 Press the larger ball of dough into a face shape about ½" thick. To make the eyes and mouth twist a pencil into the face.

3 Break the remaining dough in half and shape a nose and a moustache. Use a little water to lightly wet the back of each piece and position onto the face.

! 4 Bake in a preheated oven on a greased baking sheet at 250°F for 3—4 hours until firm. When cool, paint and varnish.

5 Cut an eye patch and band from the felt. Position on the face and secure with glue at the back of the head.

6 Make an earring by twisting a pipe cleaner into a circle. Glue to the side of the pirate's head.

7 Wrap the fabric around the pirate's head and secure on one side with the other pipe cleaner. Glue the finished head onto a long piece of ribbon.

Hang the completed faces over your closet or bedroom doors. You could model smaller faces and hang these from drawers.

A Christmas Decoration

To color the salt dough, simply follow the recipe on page 44, but add 1 tablespoon of red food coloring to the mixing water.

Materials

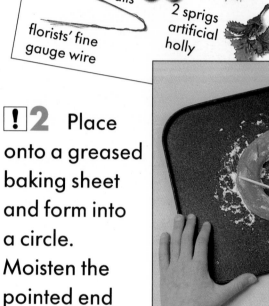

glitter

wide red ribbon

red salt dough

narrow red ribbon

2 satin-wrapped balls

2 sprigs artificial holly

tinsel

florists' fine gauge wire

1 On a lightly floured board, roll the salt dough into a thick sausage shape about 12" long. Make a hole with a pencil at one end of the sausage and model the other end into a point.

!2 Place onto a greased baking sheet and form into a circle. Moisten the pointed end and put into the hole. Smooth the join. Score the top of the ring with a plastic knife. Bake in a preheated oven for 3–4 hours at 250°F until firm, turning occasionally. Set aside to cool.

3 Lightly spread glue across the top of the dough circle and sprinkle on the glitter. Stick tinsel around the edge.

4 Thread the satin-wrapped balls onto the florists' wire. Twist the wire to keep them in place. Position the satin-wrapped balls on the bottom edge of the circle and secure by firmly winding the wire around the dough circle.

5 To hide the wire, wrap the wide ribbon between the satin-wrapped balls and tie into a bow. Glue the ends of the holly sprigs and tuck into the bow.

6 Thread the narrow ribbon through the top of the circle and knot to make a loop for hanging up the decoration. Tie the ribbon ends into a bow.

49

Pots of Fun

The models on the next few pages have been made using air-hardening clay. This will need to be left for a few days in a cool, dry place. But the end results will be well worth the wait!

1 Take 2 small lumps of clay and shape into balls between the palms of your hands.

2 Flatten the balls with your fingers.

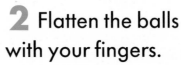

3 Use a pastry cutter to cut out a circle from each for the base and the lid of the pot. Use a round-ended knife to cut away the rough edges of the circles.

4 Roll out a sausage approximately ¼" thick and long enough to fit around the inside edge of one of the circles. Roll another 4 sausages of the same length and thickness.

50

5 Trim each end of the sausges with a diagonal cut. Now wet and gently press together the ends of each sausage to make a perfect coil.

6 Place a coil on the inside edge of one of the circles. Build up the pot by wetting and placing the remaining coils on top of each other.

You can have lots of fun decorating the pots and the lids.

STORAGE TIP
Once opened you can stop the clay from drying out by wrapping it in foil or plastic wrap and storing it in a plastic bag.

7 To make the pot lid, roll a small ball of clay and place in the center of the second circle. Leave the pot and lid to harden in a cool, dry place for several days. Paint and varnish.

A Woodland Scene

This collection of clay animals will bring a touch of nature to your bedroom. If you run out of clay, you could use salt dough instead.

The spider

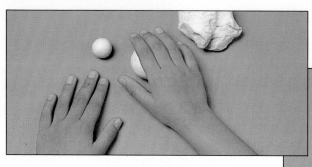

1 Roll out 2 balls of clay, a large one for the body and a small one for the head.

Materials

pine-cones, leaves and tree bark

air-hardening clay

felt

glitter

used matchstick

pipe cleaners

2 Push the used matchstick into the body, leaving about ½" sticking out. Push on the head.

3 Use a toothpick to mark hairs over the body and the head.

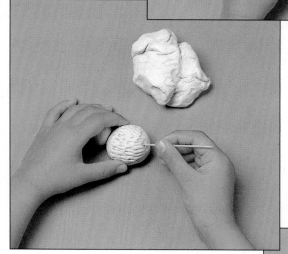

The ladybug

4 Take a small ball of clay and model it into a ladybug shape. Use a toothpick to mark in the head and the wings.

The snail

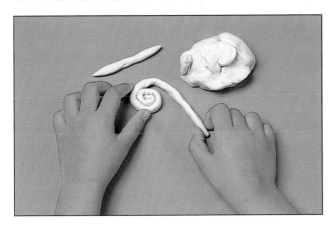

5 Roll a long and a short sausage from the clay. Roll up the long sausage into a coil and place on the shorter sausage.

6 Use a toothpick to mark in the snail's eyes and mouth, and to decorate the shell.

7 Leave the clay animals to dry for several days, then paint and varnish them. Glue 8 pipe cleaner legs to the underside of the spider and 6 to the ladybug. Stick 8 black felt spots to the ladybug's back. Glue glitter on the spider's head.

Make a woodland scene on green cardboard to display your clay animals. Decorate with stones, pinecones, leaves, dried flowers and tree bark.

53

Lighthouse Picture

Make this great picture for your bedroom wall. You can use salt dough instead of clay if you prefer.

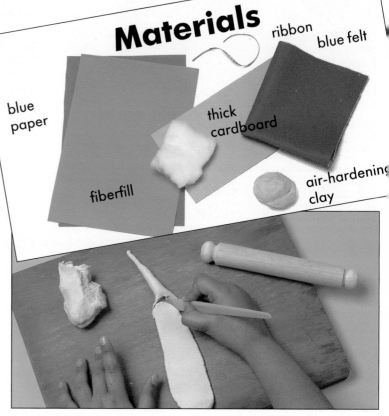

Materials

ribbon

blue felt

blue paper

thick cardboard

fiberfill

air-hardening clay

1 Roll some clay into a long sausage, thicker at one end than the other. Flatten using a rolling-pin.

2 Use a round-ended knife or modeling tool to cut out a lighthouse shape from the flattened clay.

3 Mark in the lantern house, windows and doors.

4 Shape the leftover clay into jagged rocks. Lay all the clay pieces onto a plastic wrap-covered board and leave to harden for several days in a cool, dry place.

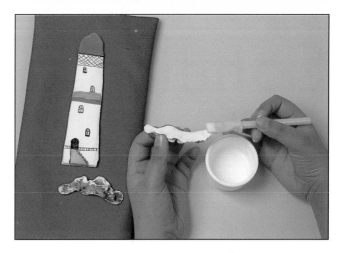

5 Paint the rocks brown and the lighthouse white. Once the paint has dried, use felt-tip pens to mark in details on the lighthouse.

6 Cut a piece of cardboard 11" x 5½" and cover with the felt. Stick the lighthouse in the center of the cardboard. Position the rocks below the lighthouse and glue in place.

7 Cut wave shapes from blue paper and glue in place below the lighthouse and around the rocks. Stick fiberfill clouds in the sky.

8 Punch 2 holes at the top of the cardboard and thread a ribbon through for hanging up the picture.

Cone People

Papier-mâché simply means 'mashed paper.' You can model it into any shape with your hands or by applying it to a mold. But it is a messy business and rubber gloves may be a good idea.

Materials

⅔ cup water

2 heaped tablespoons all-purpose flour

newspaper

feather

yarn
scraps of felt

yellow felt

1 Tear the newspaper into lengths about 1¼" wide. Tear these strips again into small pieces about 1¼" square. Put into a container.

! **2** Cover the torn paper with hot water and leave to soak overnight.

3 Take handfuls of paper and squeeze the water out. Place the squeezed-out paper into another bowl. Empty the water from the container.

4 Put the flour in the mixing cup. Add the water slowly and mix to a smooth, creamy paste.

5 Put the squeezed paper back into the container a little at a time, mixing it with small amounts of paste until it becomes a smooth pulp. You may need to mix more paste.

6 Take a handful of papier-mâché and shape into a cone. Smooth the sides. Leave to dry in a warm, dry place for several days.

7 Paint the cone with 2 coats of bright paint. When dry, paint on the eyes, nose and mouth.

8 Glue some short strands of yarn around the sides and back of the head, about 1 ½" from the top of the cone. Cut out felt in the shape of a doughnut large enough to fit over the top of the cone just above the hair. Add a feather.

If you cannot make a cone shape, make one that is rounded at the top instead, just like the little red model on the end.

Papier-Mâché Boat

A plastic bottle cut in half makes a perfect mold for making the hull of a boat from mashed paper.

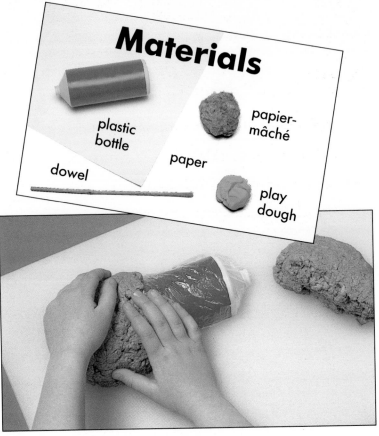

Materials

plastic bottle

papier-mâché

paper

dowel

play dough

1 Cut a small plastic bottle in half lengthwise. Cover one half with plastic wrap.

2 Spread papier-mâché evenly over the half bottle mold until it is about 1/4" thick. Leave to dry in a warm, dry place for several days.

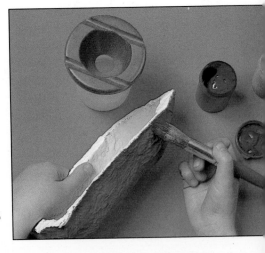

3 Carefully ease the bottle and plastic wrap from the papier-mâché. Leave for another day or two to let the inside dry out thoroughly.

4 Paint the boat inside and out. Several coats of paint may be needed. Once the paint has dried, the hull can be varnished.

58

5 To make a sail, cut a piece of paper 9½" x 8" and decorate with felt-tip pens.

6 Punch a hole at the center top and center bottom of the sail. Slip the sail onto the dowel.

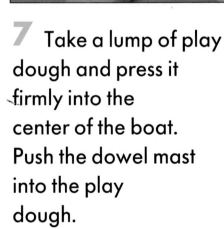

7 Take a lump of play dough and press it firmly into the center of the boat. Push the dowel mast into the play dough.

To make your boat into a Viking ship, cut out and decorate some paper circles for shields. Stick them along each side of the boat.

59

Papier-Mâché Plate

Materials

2 heaped tablespoons all-purpose flour

⅓ cup water

small paper plate

magazine pictures

newspaper torn into 1¼" strips

You can make this beautiful plate from just a few old newspapers and magazines.

1 Place the flour into a mixing cup. Gradually add the water to it to mix to a smooth, slightly runny paste.

2 Cover the front of the plate with petroleum jelly. Put a layer of newspaper strips on top. Paste well, smoothing down the paper with your fingers.

3 Lay a second layer of newspaper strips over the first layer, but in the opposite direction. Continue pasting and adding layers of newspaper strips first in one direction, then the other, until 8 layers have been completed.

4 Leave to harden for several days in a cool, dry place. When completely dry, trim the edge with scissors to neaten. Then remove the papier-mâché carefully from the plate.

To make this sun mobile, cut the edges of the papier-mâché plate into sun ray shapes. Add a circle of beads and buttons to the center and glue firmly in place.

5 Paint the back of the plate. You may need several coats to cover the newspaper.

[!] Spray the front and back with gold paint. Make sure to have an adult with you when spraying paint.

6 Decorate the front of the plate by gluing on magazine pictures.

7 Paint a light varnish over the finished plate.

Plaster Eggs

Modeling plaster or plaster of Paris as it is often known is used to make these decorative eggs.

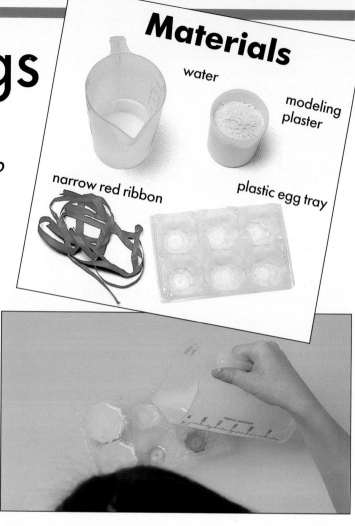

Materials

water

modeling plaster

narrow red ribbon

plastic egg tray

1 Wipe the inside of the egg tray with dishwashing liquid.

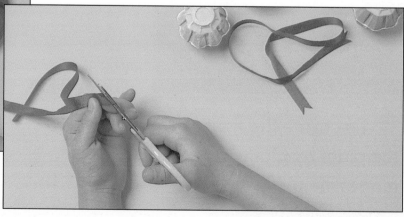

2 Mix 2 cups of plaster to 1 cup of water. Pour the liquid plaster into the egg tray. Allow to dry and harden for about an hour.

3 Remove the half egg shapes from the tray and paint. Glue 2 painted halves together.

4 Cut the ribbon into six 20" lengths and three 10" lengths.

5 Wrap a long piece of ribbon around the egg and tie in a knot at the top.

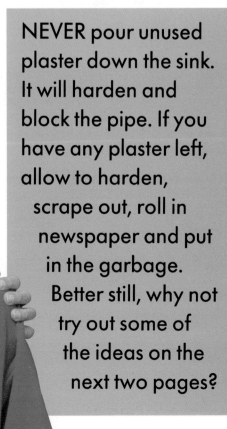

6 Tie a second long piece of ribbon around the egg and secure with a knot. Knot the ends of both ribbons together so that the egg can be hung up.

7 Take a short piece of ribbon and tie into a decorative bow at the top of the egg.

NEVER pour unused plaster down the sink. It will harden and block the pipe. If you have any plaster left, allow to harden, scrape out, roll in newspaper and put in the garbage. Better still, why not try out some of the ideas on the next two pages?

Materials

modeling plaster

play dough

toothpicks

felt

dried flowers

thin white poster board

yogurt carton

egg tray

Odds and Ends

Think twice before throwing away any plastic packaging from food products. All make excellent molds for plaster casting. Here are some simple ideas for you to try out.

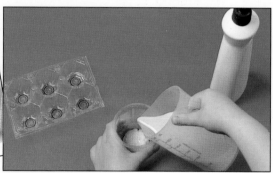

1 Wipe the insides of the plastic molds with dishwashing liquid, and fill with modeling plaster. Leave to harden, then carefully remove from the molds.

Windmill

2 Paint the yogurt cast white and an egg cast red. When this has dried, paint in doors and windows on the yogurt cast. Glue the egg cast to the top of the yogurt cast.

3 Cut out 4 sails from white poster board and decorate. Glue to the toothpick and attach to the front of the windmill with play dough.

64

Party Favors

4 Paint the remaining 5 egg casts in bright colors and leave to dry. Glue felt leaves and a dried flower to the top of each.

5 Write the names of your friends or family onto small rectangles of white poster board and stick to the bottom of each decorated cast.

Handprint Paperweight

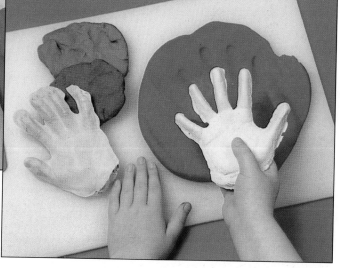

6 Roll out a large ball of play dough to about ½" thick. Firmly press your hand into the play dough. Fold up the bottom edge of the play dough if it has become flattened out. Fill the mold with plaster and leave to dry for several hours.

7 Carefully peel away the play dough from the plaster cast. Paint and varnish. Use the plaster hand to keep your drawings in place and store paper clips in the palm.

Presents

It can be just as much fun to give presents as to receive them, especially when you make them yourself. There are ideas in this section for making gifts for all your family and friends for all sorts of special occasions including birthdays, Mother's Day, Father's Day, Easter and Christmas. And almost all of these presents can be made from things that you can find around the home, such as old boxes and bits of fabric. Pictured here are some of the tools that you might need.

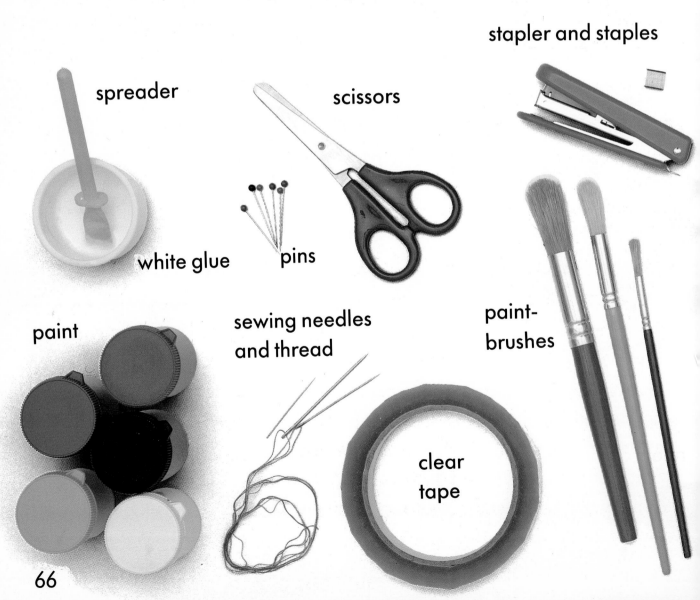

stapler and staples

spreader

scissors

white glue

pins

paint

sewing needles
and thread

paint-
brushes

clear
tape

Other Useful Things

When you begin to make presents you will find that all sorts of things come in handy. Listed below are just a few. Collect handy odds and ends in a cardboard box and keep adding to your collection.

Cardboard tubes, yogurt pots, bottle caps, jar lids, cereal boxes, matchboxes, thick poster board, paper plates, candy wrappers, tissue paper, wrapping paper, color magazines, felt, string, yarn, ribbon ends, lollipop sticks, fabric scraps, cotton spools, corks, tinsel, pipe cleaners, sequins, glitter, straws, self-adhesive shapes, pinecones, dried flowers, buttons and beads.

masking tape

tracing paper

thick poster board

craft knife

felt-tip pens

pencil sharpener

metal ruler

pencil and eraser

plastic ruler

Remember

☆ Wear an apron and cover the work area.
☆ Collect together the items in the materials box at the beginning of each project.
☆ Always ask an adult for help when you see this sign ⚠
☆ Clean up after yourself.

Teddy Bear Pencil Holder

This fun bear can be hung up on the wall or pinned onto a noticeboard.

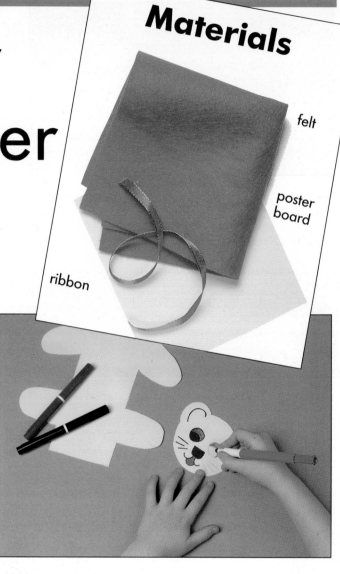

felt

poster board

ribbon

1 Trace the teddy bear templates on pages 123 and 124 onto a piece of poster board and cut out.

2 Use felt-tip pens to color in the bear's eyes, nose and mouth. Staple the head to the body.

3 Fold up the flap of poster board at the bottom of the body. Fold the legs inwards over the flap. Staple each leg to the flap to make a pocket.

4 Fold the bear's arms inwards and staple together.

68

5 Cut 2 bows from the felt and glue over the staples.

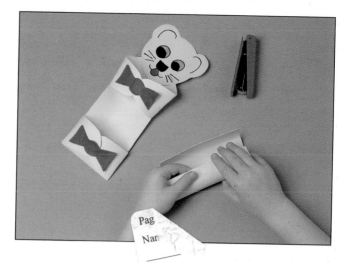

6 Cut a piece of poster board 4¾" x 6¼", roll up into a tube and staple in place.

7 Tape a ribbon loop to the back of the bear's head to hang it up with. Push the tube down between the paws.

To finish the present slip some colored pencils or felt-tip pens into the tube. For Halloween make a black cat holder. For Easter make a rabbit holder and fill it with chocolate eggs.

Butterfly Card

An unusual card that is a present too.

Materials

ribbon · safety pin · wrapping paper · foil tape · double-sided adhesive pad · thin poster board · sequins · glitter

1 Cut a piece of poster board 12" x 4¾". Fold in half.

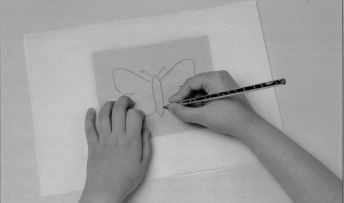

2 Trace the butterfly template (page 123) onto the front of the poster board.

3 Draw around the outline of the butterfly with a black felt-tip pen. Decorate the body.

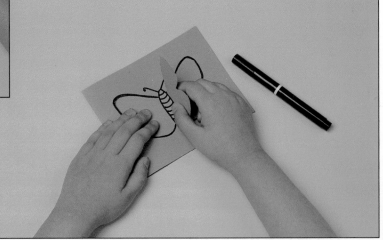

!4 Cut around the outside of the butterfly wings and lift up.

5 Cut a piece of poster board 5" x 4". Cover both sides with wrapping paper.

6 Open up the card. Tape the covered piece of poster board in place behind the lifted butterfly.

7 Trace the butterfly template onto a piece of poster board and cut out. Decorate the wings with sequins and glitter.

To finish off the card, lay a thin piece of ribbon along the folded edge and tie into a decorative bow on the outside.

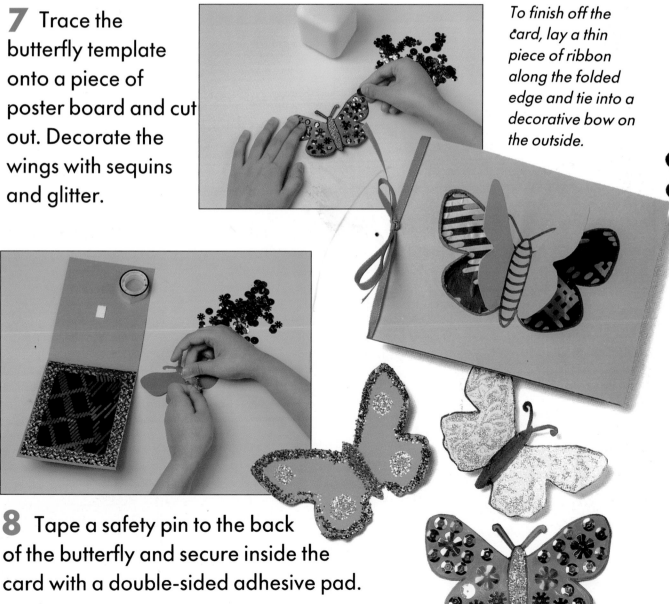

8 Tape a safety pin to the back of the butterfly and secure inside the card with a double-sided adhesive pad.

Scented Clown

Materials

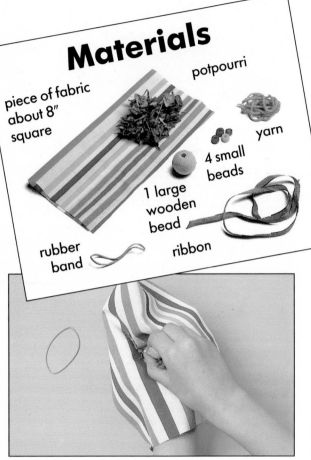

piece of fabric about 8" square

potpourri

yarn

4 small beads

1 large wooden bead

rubber band

ribbon

A colorful clown perfect for hanging in the closet to keep clothes smelling sweet.

1 Sew a bead onto each corner of the piece of fabric.

2 Put a heap of potpourri in the middle of the fabric. Gather up the edges to make a ball and fasten securely with the rubber band.

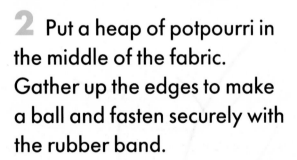

3 Paint the large wooden bead white. When it is dry, draw on a clown's face with felt-tip pens.

4 Cut 12 pieces of yarn each measuring about 2". Bundle and tie together with a piece of yarn.

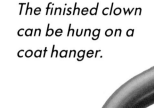
The finished clown can be hung on a coat hanger.

5 Thread yarn onto a needle and sew a couple of stitches through the back of the wig.

6 Now thread on the clown's head and sew securely onto the bag.

7 Thread a ribbon through the top of the clown's wig and knot the ends together.

73

Ollie Octopus

A perfect present for a friend to hang from the bedroom ceiling.

Materials

bulky yarn

newspaper

string

glue-on eyes

scraps of felt

crepe paper

elastic

poster board

1 Roll some newspaper into a ball and tape it into shape.

2 Cover the ball with crepe paper. Tie a piece of string tightly around the neck, leaving a ruffle.

3 Glue 2 black felt circles onto 2 larger white felt circles and glue onto the ball. Glue the eyes on top. Cut a zig zag mouth from red felt and glue on too.

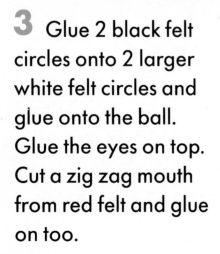

4 Cut 8 pieces of thick yarn each 10 long. Tape these eve along a strip of poste board 6" x 1¼".

74

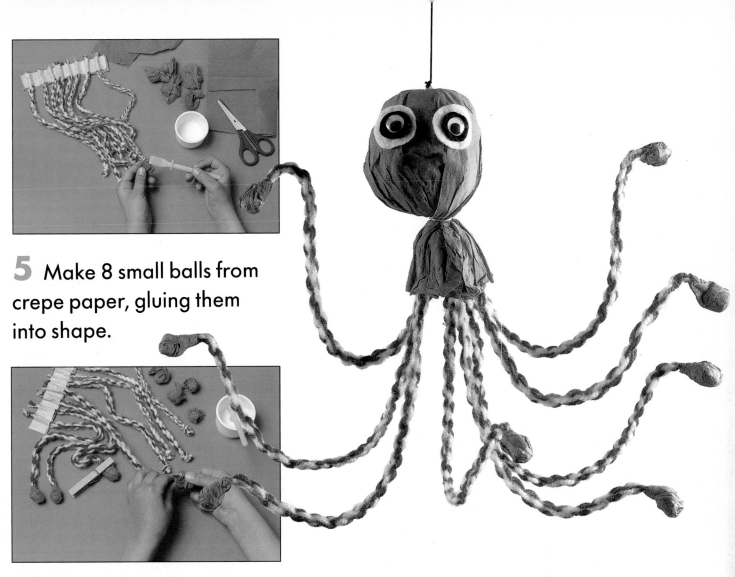

5 Make 8 small balls from crepe paper, gluing them into shape.

6 Glue a ball to the bottom of each piece of yarn.

Fasten a piece of elastic to Ollie's head so that he bounces up and down when he is hung up.

7 Tape the poster board strip into a circle and glue it inside the ruffle of the neck.

OTHER IDEAS
For a Halloween gift
Make a spider out of black paper and use pipe cleaners for the legs.
For a gift for a newborn baby
Use pastel colors and securely sew balls to the ends of the yarn.

Materials

wrapping paper

dishwashing-liquid bottle

strips of crepe paper

box

6 floral sticks

colored poster board

Ringo

Make this game for a brother or sister, then play it together to see who can get the best score.

1 Choose a wrapping paper with a repeat pattern and cut out 6 figures from it. Glue these onto thin poster board and cut around the outline.

2 Tape each figure to the top of a floral stick.

3 Cover the box with wrapping paper.

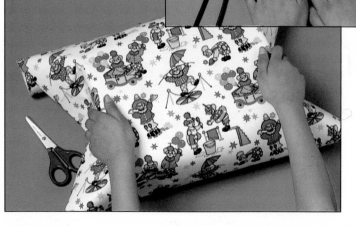

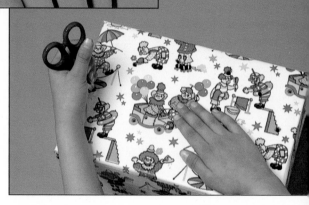

!4 Poke 6 holes through the top of the box, spacing them out evenly.

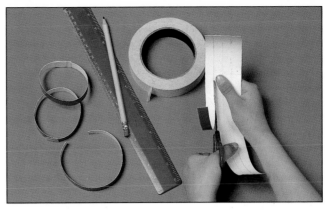

5 Use a coin or small bottle lid to draw 6 circles onto colored poster board. Cut out and number them 1 to 6. Glue a number next to each hole.

6 Cut open a dishwashing-liquid bottle. Cut six ½" strips from the plastic. Tape the strips into rings.

7 Wind the strips of crepe paper around the rings until the plastic is completely covered. Secure the ends of the paper with tape.

Push the sticks into the holes. Take turns to see how many figures you can ring. The first one to reach 50 is the winner.

77

Wizard Birthday Pin

Make this great pin for a friend to wear on his or her birthday.

Materials

felt

wooden clothespin

safety pin

thin poster board

self-adhesive stars

fiberfill

1 Mark in a face on the head of the clothespin with felt-tip pens.

2 Cut a piece of black felt 6" x 3½". Sew a line of running stitches up one long edge, leaving about 4" of thread at each end.

3 Pull both ends of the thread to gather up the felt. Put the dress around the clothespin's neck and tie securely at the back

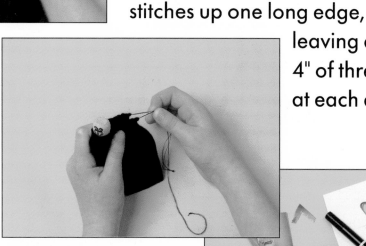

4 Cut 2 arms from white poster board and glue onto the dress. Cut a number (the age of your friend) from the gold poster board and glue onto the front of the dress.

5 Cut a piece of purple felt 3" x 3" and sew a line of running stitches along one edge. Gather the stitches.

6 Put the cloak over the dress and tie securely at the front of the wizard's neck. Decorate with stars.

7 Cut a circle of blue poster board and fold into 4. Cut along one fold line to the middle. Put glue along one cut edge and slide under the other to make a cone shape. Decorate with stars.

8 Glue some fiberfill onto the head for the hair and a beard and stick the hat on top. Attach a safety pin to the back of the cloak.

For Halloween make a clothespin doll witch and give her a broom to hold.

Elephant Memo Clip

The perfect present for a busy parent.

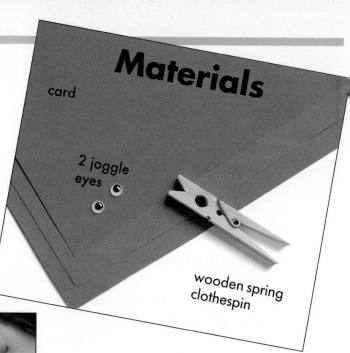

Materials

card

2 joggle eyes

wooden spring clothespin

1 Trace the elephant templates on page 124 onto stiff cardboard. You will need 2 bodies, 2 ears and 1 trunk.

2 Cut out and decorate with paint and felt-tip pens.

3 Glue the clothespin between the front and back of the elephant's body so that it sticks out at the top by about ½". Leave to dry.

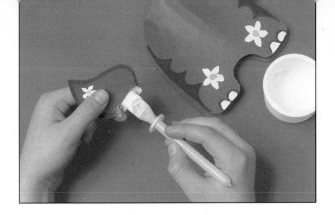

4 Glue the ears behind the front of the body. Leave to dry.

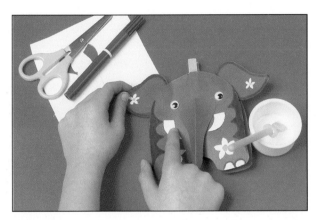

6 Stick on the glue-on eyes. Draw and cut out 2 tusks from white poster board. Glue these on either side of the trunk.

5 Make a fold down the middle of the trunk. Glue onto the center of the elephant's face.

If you use a bulldog clip instead of a clothespin, the memo clip can be hung on a pin. You can vary the design too.

Funny Face Kite

Make 2 of these and fly them with a friend.

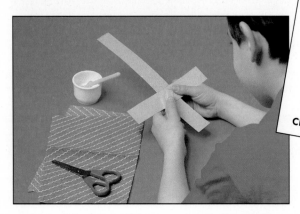

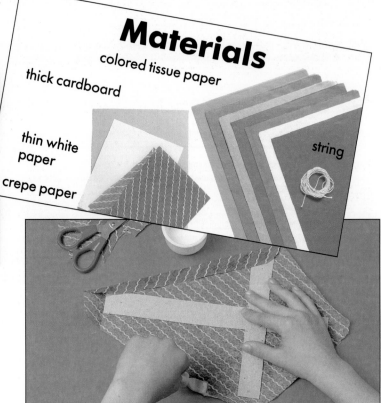

Materials

colored tissue paper

thick cardboard

thin white paper

crepe paper

string

1 Cut 2 strips of cardboard measuring 10¼" x ¾" and 6¾" x ¾". Staple into a cross. Glue the cardboard cross onto a large piece of crepe paper and leave to dry.

2 Mark a line across each corner of the paper about ½" from the cardboard cross. Cut along these lines. Fold over the edge of the paper all the way around and glue down.

3 To strengthen the cross stick pieces of masking tape over it.

4 Cut out and color 2 eyes, a nose and a mouth. Glue onto the front of the kite.

82

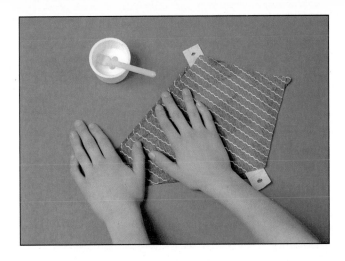

5 Fold a piece of masking tape into a square and cut a hole in the center of it. Make 3. Tape the squares to the side and bottom corners of the kite.

6 Cover the back of the kite with a piece of crepe paper cut to fit and glued in place.

7 Cut 3 pieces of string each 8" long. Tie a piece through each corner square and knot the ends together. Tie a small ball of string to the knotted-up ends.

To make a tail for the kite, cut a piece of string 16" long. Tie small pieces of colored tissue paper onto the string and tape it to the bottom of the kite. Thread long strips of colored tissue paper through the side holes to make tassels.

83

Photo Frame

Put a picture of yourself in this present and give it to your grandparents.

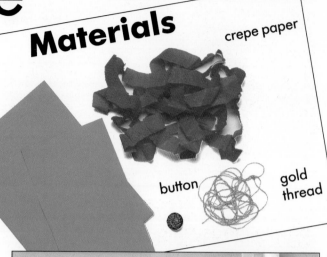

Materials

thick poster board

crepe paper

button

gold thread

1 Cut out 2 pieces of poster board each measuring 8" x 6¼". Draw a line as wide as your ruler all the way around one piece of poster board. Cut out the middle space.

2 Wind ¾" wide strips of crepe paper around the poster board frame, fixing in place with a dab of glue here and there.

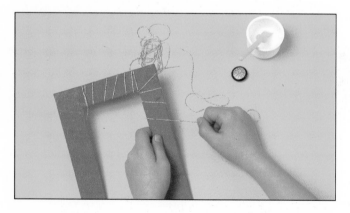

3 Tie the gold thread to the frame and wrap it around and around. Secure the thread with a knot at the back.

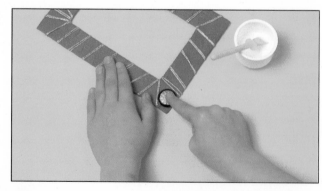

4 Glue a large button to one corner.

5 Cut out a piece of poster board measuring 5½" x 2½". Draw a line ¾" in from the edge. Score along the line and gently bend back.

6 Glue the support arm onto the back poster board 4" up from the bottom edge and secure with masking tape. Leave under a weight to dry.

7 Put glue along 3 sides of the back poster board leaving the top edge unglued. Press the covered frame onto it and leave under a weight to dry.

When the glue has dried, you can slip a photo of yourself into the frame.

Flower Cart

The perfect present for Mother's Day.

small cardboard box

thin blue card

thin white card

Materials

coloured tissue-paper

1 Put the box on a sheet of tissue paper. Push the paper over the edges of the box and secure with glue.

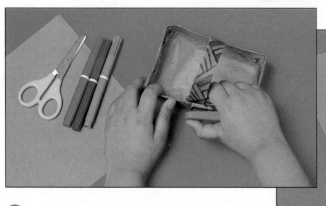

2 Cut a strip of blue poster board 7" x ¾". Decorate with felt-tip pens.

3 Staple the decorated strip of poster board to the box to make a handle.

4 To make an awning for the cart, cut a piece of blue poster board 4" x 3½". Decorate with stripes.

86

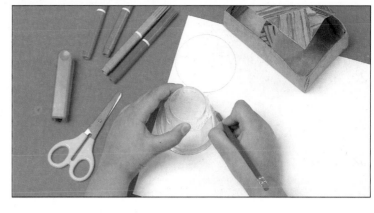

5 Fold the poster board in half and staple to the handle.

6 Use a yogurt carton to draw 2 circles onto white poster board. Cut out. Draw in the spokes and staple to either side of the cart.

The flower cart, brimming with tissue paper flowers, will make a beautiful table or windowsill decoration.

7 Crumple up some green tissue paper and fill the cart with it. Cut out flower shapes from colored tissue paper and glue onto the green base. Stick small balls of colored tissue paper in the center of the flower shapes.

Eggs in a Basket

A colorful surprise for Easter Day!

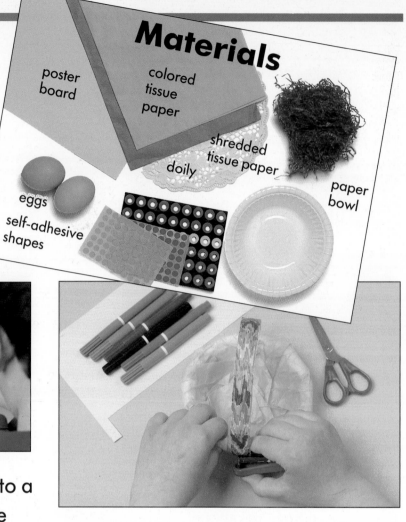

Materials

poster board

colored tissue paper

shredded tissue paper

doily

eggs

self-adhesive shapes

paper bowl

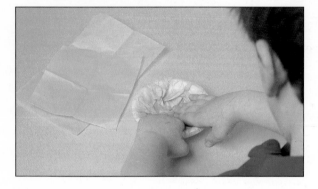

1 Place the paper bowl onto a piece of tissue paper. Pull the paper over the edges of the bowl and smooth down.

2 Cut a strip of poster board, decorate and staple to the bowl.

3 Glue a thin strip of blue tissue paper around the bowl. Glue pieces cut from the doily to the rim of the bowl. Fill with shredded tissue paper.

4 Make a hole at the top of an egg with a sewing needle. Make a larger hole at the bottom.

5 Hold the egg over a bowl and blow through the smaller hole until the egg is empty. Carefully rinse and drain the egg.

6 When the egg is dry cover the holes with masking tape. Paint the egg all over.

Place the decorated eggs in the basket on a nest of shredded tissue paper. Scatter small sugar or chocolate eggs all around. You could make a gift tag from poster board and tie it on to the handle.

7 When the paint is dry, decorate the egg with self-adhesive shapes.

89

Egg and Chick Mobile

Make this beautiful springtime gift.

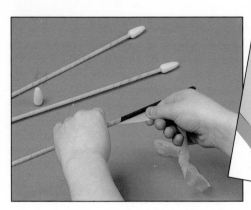

Materials

yellow and white poster board

yellow cotton balls

strips of crepe paper

3 floral sticks

string

ribbon

8 glue-on eyes

7 beads

gold thread

1 Wrap strips of crepe paper around the floral sticks and push a bead onto each end.

! 2 Make a star shape out of the decorated sticks. Tie in the middle with the string.

3 Draw 4 chick and 8 wing shapes onto yellow poster board using the templates on page 123. Cut out.

4 Glue yellow cotton balls, wings and glue-on eyes onto both sides of each chick.

90

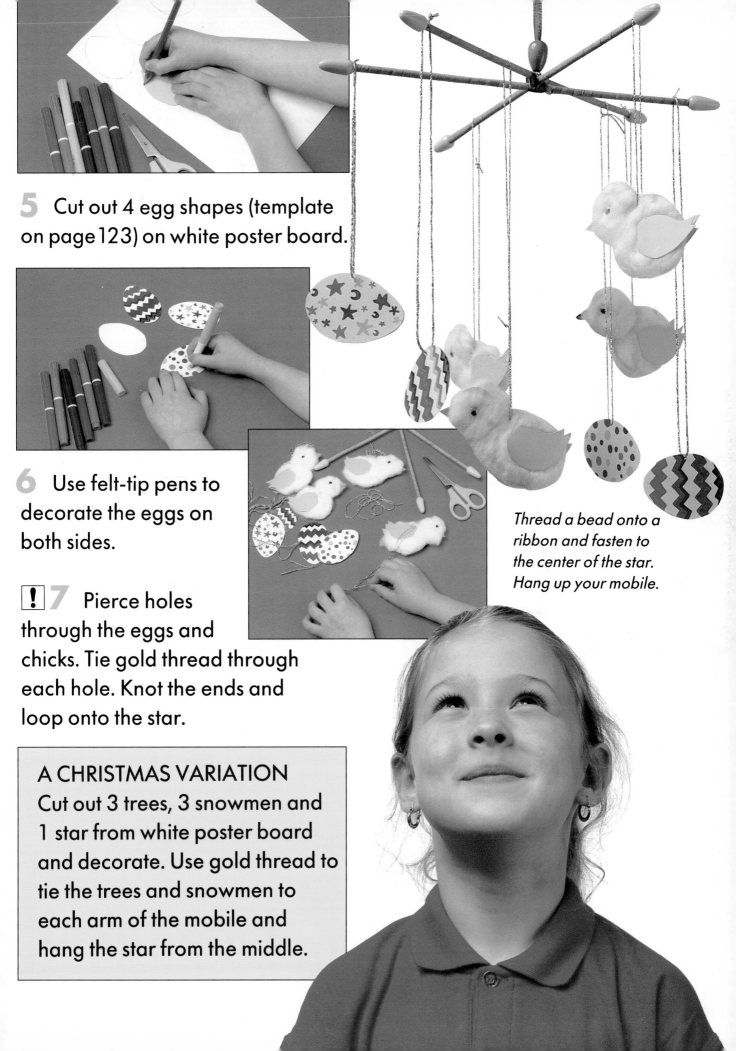

5 Cut out 4 egg shapes (template on page 123) on white poster board.

6 Use felt-tip pens to decorate the eggs on both sides.

!7 Pierce holes through the eggs and chicks. Tie gold thread through each hole. Knot the ends and loop onto the star.

Thread a bead onto a ribbon and fasten to the center of the star. Hang up your mobile.

A CHRISTMAS VARIATION
Cut out 3 trees, 3 snowmen and 1 star from white poster board and decorate. Use gold thread to tie the trees and snowmen to each arm of the mobile and hang the star from the middle.

Mini Felt Stockings

The perfect present for the Christmas tree.

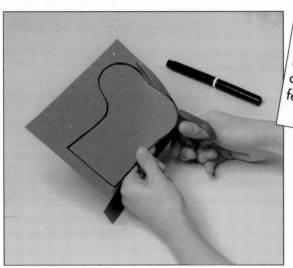

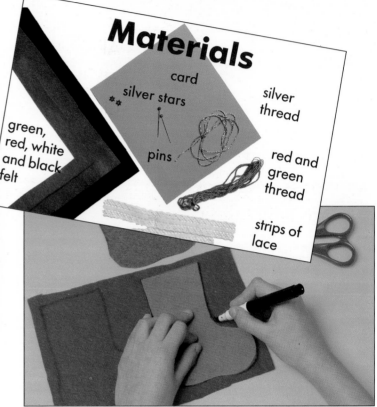

Materials

card

silver stars

green, red, white and black felt

pins

silver thread

red and green thread

strips of lace

1 Trace the stocking on page 124 onto poster board and cut out to make a template.

2 Draw around the stocking template twice on the red felt and twice on the green felt. Cut out. Pin the red stockings together and the green stockings together.

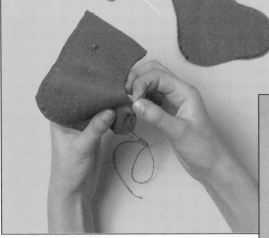

3 Sew an even line of running stitches around the stockings, leaving the tops open.

4 Cut 2 small pieces of lace to fit around the top of the stockings. Glue in place.

5 Cut 2 snowmen from white felt (template on page 124) and glue to the stockings. Mark faces and buttons with felt-tip pens.

6 Cut 2 hats from black felt (template page 124) and glue in place. Stick a silver star above the snowmen.

7 Sew a loop of silver thread through the top of each stocking. They can be hung from a tree and filled with small presents.

Make several stockings, one for each member of your family, and decorate each with a different Christmas design.

Jewelry

This section is full of exciting ideas for turning junk into beautiful jewelry. Some of the projects are quick to make and can be finished in one session, Bottle Bracelets (page 100) and Robin Hood Pouch (page 108) to name just two. Some of the other projects can't be finished in one session. You will have to be patient as you wait for paint to dry, dough to bake or varnish to set. It's a good idea to work on two or more projects at a time, so that you can be getting on with something while you are waiting. Before starting work on any of the projects in this section, do make sure that you have all the tools that you will need as pictured here.

modeling tool

white glue and spreader

felt-tip pens

paint

paint-brushes

needles

double-sided tape

rolling pin

pins

masking tape

clear tape

Other Useful Things

All sorts of things come in useful for making jewelry. Start a collection and keep adding to it. Store handy odds and ends in a box. Your collection might include:

Plastic bottles, textured plastic packaging, cardboard tubes, yogurt cartons, bottle caps, jar lids, old newspapers, corrugated cardboard, colored poster board and colored paper, gold and silver poster board, gummed paper, crepe paper, tissue paper, yarn, string, gold and silver thread, elastic, cellophane and foil candy wrappers, broken bead necklaces, tinsel, glitter, self-adhesive stickers, buttons, sequins, felt, fabric scraps, barrettes, hairbands, safety pins.

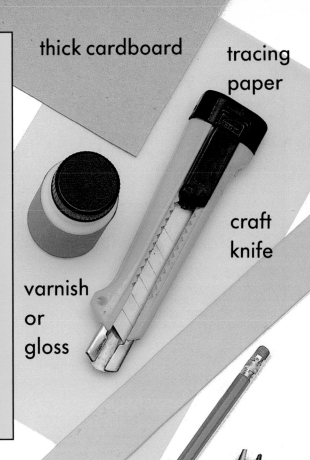

thick cardboard

tracing paper

craft knife

varnish or gloss

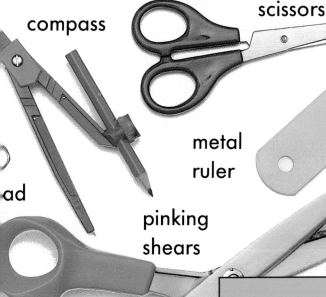

compass

scissors

metal ruler

ad

pinking shears

pencil and eraser

pliers

ruler

Remember

☆ Wear an apron and cover the work area.
☆ Collect together the items in the materials box at the beginning of each project.
☆ Always ask an adult for help when you see this sign ⚠
☆ Clean up after yourself.

95

Cork Beads

Save up used corks to make this beautiful necklace. Alternatively, corks can be cheaply bought from stores that sell wine-making equipment.

Materials

metal hooks and eyes

12 corks

1 Hold the corks at each end and paint using about 3 different base colors. Stand the painted corks on one end, paint the other end and leave to dry. Turn over and paint the other end the same color.

2 Decorate the painted corks with patterns in contrasting colors making them as bright as you can. Leave to dry.

3 Lightly varnish the painted corks and leave to dry.

4 Screw a hook and an eye into either end of 9 of the corks.

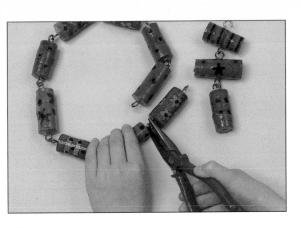
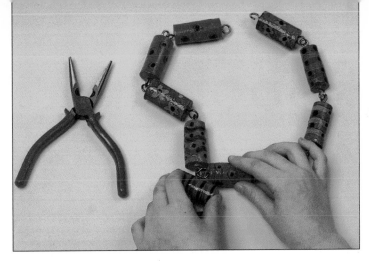

5 Join these 9 corks together. Use pliers to close up the hooks, but leave the last hook open so that the necklace can be put on easily.

6 Make a pendant by joining together the remaining 3 corks. Hook the pendant onto the necklace.

TO MAKE THE BRACELET
Cut several corks into 3 pieces each. Paint and varnish. Thread a piece of yarn or thin elastic through a sewing needle. Push the needle through the center of a cork bead, thread on a brightly-colored wooden bead, add another cork bead, then another wooden bead, and so on until the bracelet is long enough to fit your wrist. Unthread the needle and tie the ends of elastic into a knot, and trim back the ends.

Robot Pins

An opportunity to use lots of bits and pieces — collect anything silver and gold and create your own robotic characters.

Materials

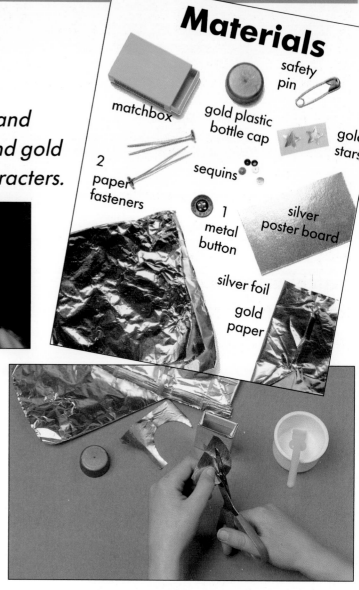

matchbox

gold plastic bottle cap

safety pin

gold stars

sequins

2 paper fasteners

1 metal button

silver poster board

silver foil

gold paper

1 Cover a matchbox with silver foil leaving one end unwrapped. Pull down the cardboard flap at the open end and cut off. Push the matchbox back in.

2 Cut a semicircle of gold paper. Cut a fringe along the curved edge.

3 Glue the fringed semicircle onto the back of the bottle cap. Glue 2 sequins inside the bottle cap to make the robot's eyes.

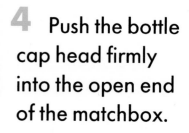

4 Push the bottle cap head firmly into the open end of the matchbox.

98

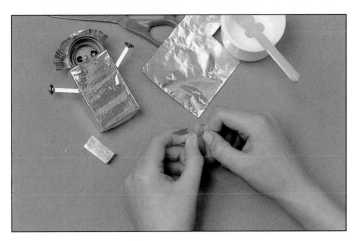

[!] **5** Use a scissor blade to make a small slit a third of the way down each side of the matchbox. Push a long paper fastener into each hole to make the robot's arms.

6 To make the robot's legs cut 2 pieces of thin silver poster board ½" x 1¼" and fold over ½" to make the feet. Glue to the back of the matchbox.

7 Decorate the front of the robot with the stars, sequins and button.

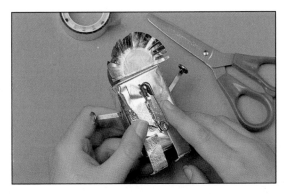

8 Tape a safety pin to the back of the robot and it is ready to wear.

Make a robot from a large matchbox which can be opened to keep small treasures in.

99

Bottle Bracelets

Recycle plastic bags and bottles to make these stunning bracelets. Wash out the bottles thoroughly first, and soak off the labels in warm, soapy water.

Materials

plastic bottles

plastic bags

yarn

cardboard

⚠ 1 Cut a 1½" wide band from a round plastic bottle. Trim the edges with scissors. Try it on over your hand — if it is too big, cut and re-join with tape to fit.

2 Cut a plastic bag into strips about 2½" wide.

3 Wind the strips around the plastic band securing each piece with a small piece of tape, until the bracelet looks well-padded.

4 To make the pom pom, cut 2 discs from cardboard measuring 2½" in diameter with a ½" hole in the center.

5 Cut striped plastic bags into thin strips. Wrap these around the cardboard 'doughnut' until there are several layers of plastic covering it.

6 Use a pair of scissors to cut through the plastic along the edge of the cardboard rings.

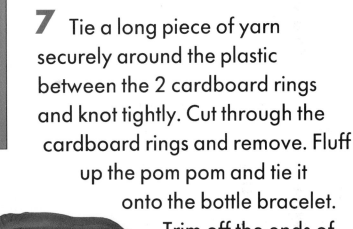

7 Tie a long piece of yarn securely around the plastic between the 2 cardboard rings and knot tightly. Cut through the cardboard rings and remove. Fluff up the pom pom and tie it onto the bottle bracelet. Trim off the ends of the yarn.

Autumn Leaf Necklace

A seasonal necklace from pieces of cardboard and a few beads.

Materials

9 wooden beads

corrugated cardboard

yarn

1 Trace the leaf templates on page 125 and draw 3 of each onto the corrugated cardboard. Cut out.

2 Paint the leaves on both sides, using about 3 different base colors. Leave to dry.

3 Paint vein patterns onto the leaves in contrasting colors and leave to dry.

4 Lightly varnish the leaves on one side. Leave to dry, then turn over and varnish the other side.

5 Thread some yarn onto a sewing needle, making sure that it is long enough to go over your head. Push the needle through the back of the leaf close to the top edge. Thread on a bead, then push the needle back out through the front of the leaf.

6 Continue to thread on the leaves and the beads. When they are all threaded on, make sure there is an equal amount of yarn at each end and knot the ends together.

You could also make a summer shell necklace using the templates on page 125, threaded together with pearls rather than beads.

103

Materials

12 large pasta tubes

feathers

8 beads

self-adhesive dots

large plastic container with rim

string

red and yellow poster board

Apache Fun

A tooth necklace and feather armband that are perfect for dressing up.

Tooth necklace

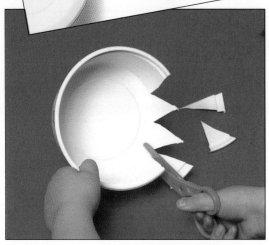

1 Cut 7 triangular 'teeth' from a large plastic container cutting down from the rim.

2 Thread the beads onto a long piece of string. Run some glue under the rim of a tooth and stick onto the string between the middle 2 beads.

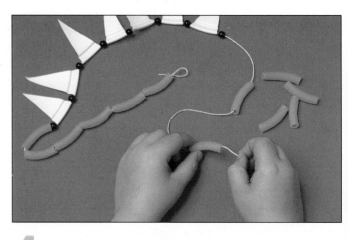

3 Continue to glue the teeth between the beads until they have all been used.

4 Thread 6 large pasta tubes onto either side of the string and knot the ends of the string together.

Feather armband

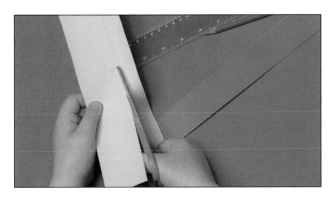

5 Cut a piece of red poster board 1½" wide and long enough to go around your upper arm including a 1½" overlap. Cut a strip of yellow poster board the same length and ¾" wide.

6 Use pinking shears to cut out a zig zag along one edge of the yellow poster board and glue onto the red poster board. Glue black dots on each of the yellow triangles.

7 Cut off a long piece of black and/or white string and glue onto the red poster board following the zig zag pattern of the yellow poster board. Turn the poster board over and tape feathers along the bottom (string) edge. *You could make a feather headband too. Use double-sided tape to join the ends of the headband or armband.*

Snake Charmers

SSSSsensational snakes to slither up your arms or hook over your ears.

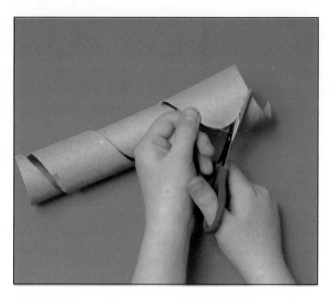

Snake armband

1 Cut the cardboard tube into a spiral about 2" wide. Straighten out gently and trim the edges with scissors.

2 Cut one end rounded for the head. Leave the other end pointed for the tail.

3 Paint the outside of the spiral green and leave to dry.

4 Tear the gummed paper into strips and use to decorate the spiral. Fold the ends of the paper over the edges of the cardboard.

5 Glue small dots all over the snake's body to decorate. Glue 2 large dots onto the head for eyes and glue sequins into the center of them.

Ear snake

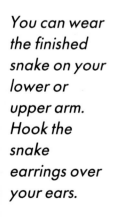

6 Trace 2 snakes onto white poster board using the template on page 125. Cut out and paint.

7 Decorate with self-adhesive dots.

You can wear the finished snake on your lower or upper arm. Hook the snake earrings over your ears.

Robin Hood Pouch

A simple-to-make money bag that can be hung from your belt or around your neck.

Materials

green felt

40" of cord

large wooden bead

painted cardboard leaf (from page 102)

1 Use a compass to draw a 9¾" diameter circle onto a piece of paper. Draw another circle within it of 8" diameter.

2 Divide the inner circle into 16 equal sections.

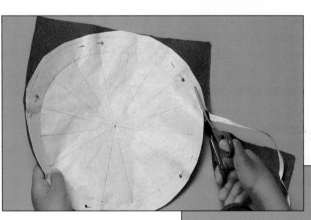

3 Roughly trim down the paper around the circle and pin onto the felt. Cut around the outer circle.

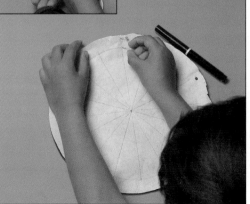

4 Before unpinning the paper, poke a pin through each of the 16 points marked on the inner circle and mark with a pen dot on the felt. Unpin the paper.

5 Fold in half along each of the marked dots in turn and cut tiny slits, just large enough to thread the cord through to make a drawstring.

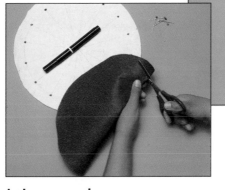

6 Begin to thread the cord through the holes. Thread on the painted leaf *(instructions for making on page 102)* between the 8th and the 9th hole.

7 When you have threaded the cord through all the holes, pull the ends together and ease the felt into a pouch shape.

8 Thread the cord ends through a snugly fitting bead and knot the ends together. To close the pouch push the bead down.

You can make a pretty party purse and decorate it with sequins and beads.

Pins For Everyone!

These bright pins are made from layers of newspaper pasted onto a shaped piece of cardboard.

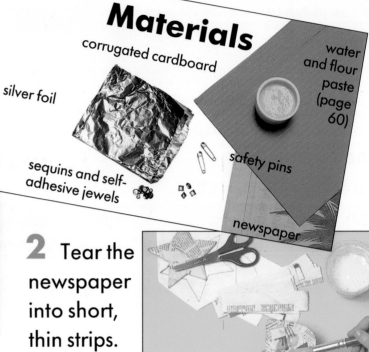

Materials

corrugated cardboard

silver foil

water and flour paste (page 60)

safety pins

sequins and self-adhesive jewels

newspaper

1 Trace the heart and star templates on page 125 onto corrugated cardboard. Cut out.

The sheriff star

3 Cover the star in silver foil, pressing carefully around the edges and gluing in place at the back.

2 Tear the newspaper into short, thin strips. Brush the shapes

lightly with paste and cover both the back and front with the strips. Put on several layers of newspaper strips, pasting in between. Leave to dry.

4 Roll 5 balls of foil and attach to the star points with tape.

The heart

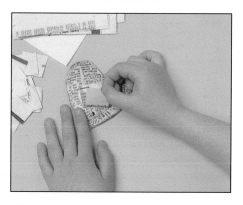

5 Add more layers of newspaper to the center of the heart to give a ballooning effect. Leave to dry.

6 Paint the base color. When this is dry, paint on patterns in contrasting colors. Once dry cover with a light coat of varnish.

7 Once the varnish has dried, stick on jewels and sequins to decorate.

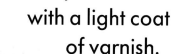

Tape safety pins to the back of the finished pins and they are ready to wear. You can also use the smaller templates on page 125 to make beautiful brooches. Decorate in the same way as the pins and tape gold thread between the decorated shapes.

111

Out of This World

Re-use old plastic bottles and packaging for effects that are out of this world.

The pin

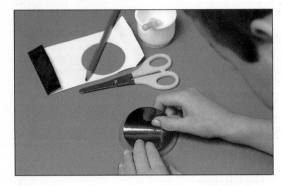

1 Cut a circle from the metallic paper to fit snugly into the plastic lid. Secure with a dab of glue.

Materials

safety pin

paper fastener

metallic paper

molded plastic

self-adhesive stars

white paper

plastic lid with lip

silver spray paint

2 large plastic bottles

2 Cut a star out of white paper and stick in the center of the metallic paper.

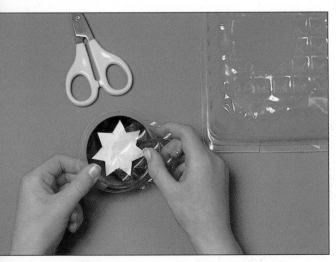

3 Cut a circle from the molded plastic to fit snugly into the plastic lid and place on top of the star.

! **4** Pierce a hole in the center of your junk sandwich with the end of a scissor blade. Push the paper fastener through the hole and open out at the back.

The gauntlets

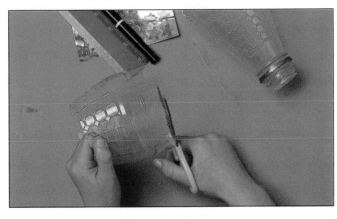

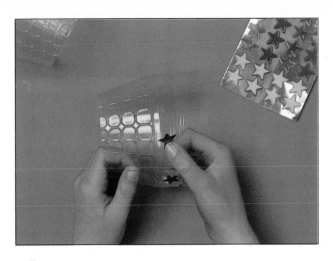

[!] **5** Mark 2 lines 3" and 6" from the neck of the bottles. Cut along these lines and trim the rough edges with scissors.

6 Stick two rows of stars around the wider end of the bottles.

Tape a safety pin to the back of the pin and pin it onto your shirt. Slip the gauntlets over your hands and prepare for blast off.

7 Spray all over with silver spray paint. When the paint has dried completely carefully remove the stars.

113

Sparkly Garland

Don't just decorate the tree this Christmas. Why not decorate yourself too?

Materials

silver and red tinsel

thin gold ribbon

40" gold string

1 Cut five 4" lengths from the silver tinsel and five 4" lengths from the red tinsel. Cut ten ¾" lengths of double-sided tape.

2 Fold each piece of tinsel in half and press a piece of double-sided tape onto it.

3 Attach a piece of silver tinsel 10" in from the end of the gold string by removing the backing from the double-sided tape and folding the tinsel around the string. Position all the silver tinsel pieces along the string about 4" apart from each other.

4 Cut eight 12" lengths from gold ribbon. Tie 2 pieces onto the gold string between each piece of silver tinsel.

5 Push the gold ribbon close to the tinsel. Curl the ribbon with closed scissor blades.

Stick colored tinsel onto barrettes, combs and hairbands to make some stunning sparkly pieces for your hair.

6 Finally add the red tinsel pieces. Remove the backing of the double-sided tape and fold onto the gold string between the gold ribbons.

7 Knot the ends of the string together.

Animal Pins

These animal pins are made from salt dough, which can be modeled into any shape you choose.

Materials

3½ oz all-purpose flour

1 ³/₄ oz salt

⅓ cup water

1 teaspoon cooking oil

safety pins

1 Mix together the salt, flour and cooking oil in a bowl. Add the water a little at a time and mix to a smooth paste.

2 Turn the dough out onto a lightly floured board. Knead and roll out to about ¼" thick. Cut out some animal shapes.

3 Add salt dough eyes, wings or fins. Model the dough, brush lightly with a little water and press down firmly onto the animal shapes.

!4 Add decorative details. Place the finished pins onto a lightly greased baking sheet and bake in the oven on the lowest setting overnight.

5 Paint the animal shapes in bright colors and leave to dry.

6 Add detail with a fine paintbrush, or felt-tip pens. Once dry, seal all over with a light coat of varnish.

Tape a safety pin to the back of the pins and they are ready to wear.

ANIMAL WALLHANGING
Make some other animal shapes — why not try zoo animals this time. Decorate and varnish them and glue them to a long piece of felt. Hang it up in your room.

Flowers For Your Hair

A corsage that will stay as fresh as the day you make it.

Materials

crepe paper (dark pink, pink, yellow, green)

green wire

safety pin

1 Mark out circles measuring about 4" in diameter onto the crepe paper. You will need 6 yellow and a total of 9 light and dark pink circles. Cut out. You can use pinking shears for decorative effect.

2 Place 3 circles of crepe paper on top of each other. Fold in half. Hold in the center and pinch together between thumb and forefinger.

3 Wind about 4" of wire around the base of the flower head. Twist the ends together and press close to the flower.

4 Cut a 2" wide strip of green crepe paper. Cut a zig zag pattern along one edge to make the leaves. Cut into sections of 4 leaves long.

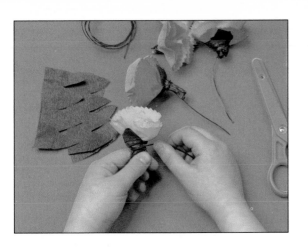

5 Wind a leaf section around the base of the flower head and secure with the end of a 6" length of wire. Leave the rest of the wire hanging down.

6 Cover the top of the wire with a piece of green crepe paper 1½" x ¾" backed with double-sided tape: remove the backing and wind around pressing firmly together.

7 Once you have made all 5 flowers, hold together in a bunch. Wind the stem of one flower around the rest to keep in place.

Attach the bunch of flowers to a hat or a piece of clothing with a safety pin fastened inside the item of clothing. Individual flowers can be wound around a hairband or hair comb for a very pretty effect.

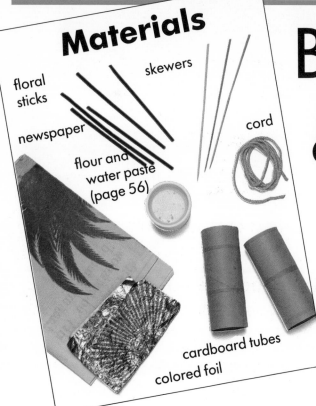

Materials

floral sticks

skewers

newspaper

cord

flour and water paste (page 56)

cardboard tubes

colored foil

Beads, Beads & More Beads

Lots of different beads to make. Thread them onto string, yarn, elastic, or even an old shoelace.

Papier-mâché beads

1 Tear newspaper into stamp-size squares and put into a bowl. Cover with warm water and leave to soak for 24 hours.

2 Squeeze the water from the paper and drain. Add a little paste and mix well to form a mush.

3 Take small balls of mush and form into large beads around the floral sticks.

!4 Slide the balls carefully off the sticks and place onto an old baking sheet. Leave in the oven overnight on its lowest setting to dry out thoroughly.

5 Thread the beads back onto the sticks. Stick the end of the sticks into a lump of play dough, making sure that the beads are not touching each other. Decorate with paint, then varnish. Slide the beads off the sticks once dry.

Paper beads

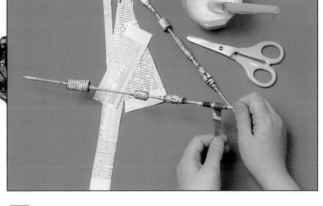

6 Cut newspaper into strips of different widths and lengths, including some pennant-shaped strips. The longer the strip the larger the bead will be.

7 Put paste on one side of the paper strips and wind glue-side down around the skewers. Gently pull the beads off the skewers and leave to dry.

Continues on next page

121

8 Thread the beads back onto the skewers and stick into a ball of play dough. Paint the beads all over and leave to dry. Use several different base colors.

9 Decorate the beads by painting on patterns in contrasting colors and by sticking on strips of colored foil. When dry, slide the beads off the skewers.

Cardboard beads

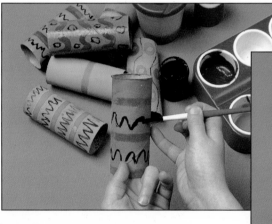

10 Paint and decorate the tubes. When dry cover with a light coat of varnish and leave to dry.

11 Cut open the tubes and paint the insides black. When dry, cut into ¾" wide sections.

12 Tape the painted sections into circles once again, linking them as you go to make a chain.

Templates

It is a good idea to make a poster board template that you can re-use time and time again. Lay a piece of tracing paper over the required template. Draw around the outline with a pencil. Turn over the tracing paper and scribble over the pencil outline. Turn the tracing paper over once again and lay down onto a piece of thick poster board. Carefully draw around the pencil outline. Remove the tracing paper. The outline of the traced shape on the poster board may be quite faint. Go over it with a black felt-tip pen. Cut out and label the poster board template and keep it in a safe place. Use the poster board template to draw around as many times as is needed onto paper, poster board or material.

Cat Pencil Holder
(alternative pages 68–69)
HEAD

Egg and
Chick Mobile
(pages 90–91)
WING

Teddy Bear Pencil
Holder
(pages 68–69)
HEAD

Egg and Chick Mobile
(pages 90–91)
CHICK

Butterfly Card
(pages 70–71)
BUTTERFLY

Egg and Chick Mobile
(pages 90–91)
EGG

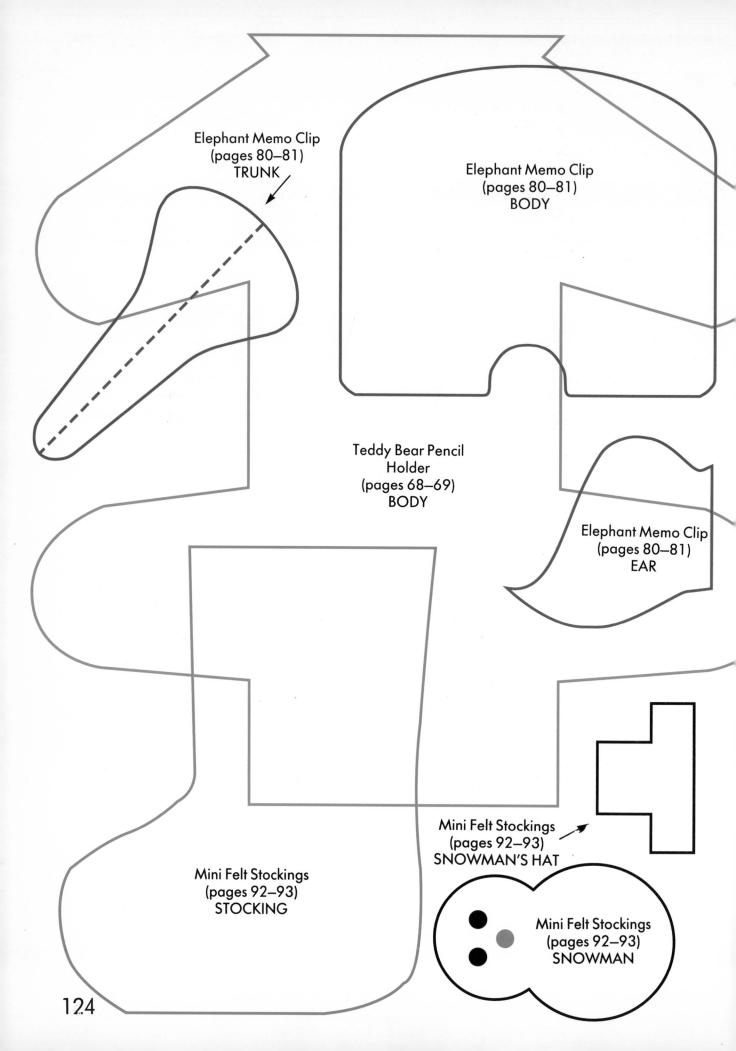

Elephant Memo Clip
(pages 80–81)
TRUNK

Elephant Memo Clip
(pages 80–81)
BODY

Teddy Bear Pencil
Holder
(pages 68–69)
BODY

Elephant Memo Clip
(pages 80–81)
EAR

Mini Felt Stockings
(pages 92–93)
SNOWMAN'S HAT

Mini Felt Stockings
(pages 92–93)
STOCKING

Mini Felt Stockings
(pages 92–93)
SNOWMAN

124

Instead, if you do not wish to make a poster board template for the project you are working on, you could trace around the required outline or outlines using tracing paper or waxed paper. Then transfer the outline onto paper or poster board as described on page 123. Remember when making a tracing you must always use a pencil; it will not work if you use a felt-tip pen.

Pins For
Everyone
(pages 110–111)
HEART

Shell Necklace
(alternative
pages 102–103)
SHELL

Pins For
Everyone
(pages 110–
111)

Shell Necklace
(alternative
pages 102–103)
SHELL

Snake Charmers
(pages 106–107)
EAR SNAKE

Autumn Leaf
Necklace
(pages 102–103)
LEAVES

Advice to Parents

The projects in this book have been broken down into a number of step-by-step instructions, each illustrated with a color photograph, so that the child can begin to tackle a range of crafts on his own. The information on the following pages has been provided to enable you to help your child to get the most from these activities.

WHAT YOU NEED TO PROVIDE

All that is required of you is an area where your child can work undisturbed, a few basic tools and readily available materials, and your interest and encouragement. Every child responds well to praise, and you are the best person to provide that. Try to keep the things your children make on display around the home to encourage them to be proud of what they have achieved.

MAKING SPACE

A table surface is not always the best place for making things; it can be very frustrating for the child to be told to clean up for dinner just as he is in the middle of something. The best solution is to lay an old sheet down on the floor in a corner of the room where the child will not be in anybody's way. Lay newspaper on top of the sheet to soak up any spills. This way, the child can safely leave his work for short periods (to allow glue or paint to dry).

CLEANING UP

You can minimize the mess by making sure the work space is well covered and by covering up your child before she begins work. Buy a wipe-clean plastic apron, or make a smock out of an old shirt — simply cut off the collar and cuffs and sew some elastic in their place.

Encourage your child to help you clean up afterwards. Wash paint jars and brushes out well so that they are ready for use next time. Store the dry brushes bristle end up in a pot or jar. Make sure felt-tip pen caps are replaced. Clean the nozzle of the glue bottle to prevent it from clogging.

MATERIALS AND TOOLS

It is important that all tools and materials provided for craft activities are simple and safe to use.

Paint

Always have the basic set of colors on hand: red, blue, yellow, black and white. All other colors can be mixed from these. Encourage your child to explore color mixing for his/herself. Provide your child with an old plate to mix paint on. Buy ready-mixed water-based paint in the economy large bottle size. These last for ages and they mix well. Always make sure that paint has dried before going on to the next step in the project.

Felt-tip Pens

A good set of felt-tip pens is ideal for decoration when the child either has no time, or is not willing, to wait for paint to dry (particularly suitable for the younger child). Felt-tip pens are available that will wash out of clothes easily in the event of an accident.

Paper and Cardboard

Always keep both white and colored paper and poster board or cardboard in the house. Paper and cardboard can be expensive to buy, so do make a point of trying to recycle materials wherever possible. Save cereal boxes, old cardboard boxes, newspapers, clothes packaging, wallpaper pieces, out-of-date calendars — anything in fact that would otherwise be thrown away. Old cereal boxes, folded flat, are perfect when thin to medium-weight cardboard is needed: simply paint the unprinted side of the cardboard whatever color is required.

Glue

Solvent-free white craft glue is recommended as it is versatile, clean, strong and safe.

Double-sided Tape

This tape is very strong and can be used as an alternative to glue for speedy results. It is expensive but if you use it carefully it will go a long way. It comes in rolls in various widths and can be bought at a stationery or art and craft store.

Scissors

For the sake of safety children should use small scissors with round-ended metal blades and plastic handles. Although these are fine for cutting paper and thin cardboard they will not cut thick cardboard and this is best done by an adult. This will often require a craft knife. Use a metal ruler to provide a straight cutting edge. If you do not have a cutting mat, use an old chopping board or very thick cardboard to protect the work surface beneath. Regularly change the craft knife blade for a clean, sharp cut. Pinking shears are fun to use as they give an interesting zig zag edge to paper and fabric.

Varnish

A light coat of varnish will give finished items a shiny finish and a protective coat that will help them to last longer. You should buy non-toxic varnish that is suitable for children to use, available from most art and craft stores. Always ensure that the varnish has completely dried before adding any decorations.

Compass

A compass is a good tool for drawing a perfect circle. The diameter of a circle is the measurement taken across its center. The compass needs to be fixed at half the measurement of the diameter. If for example a 9½" diameter circle is needed, use a ruler to measure off 4¾" between the compass point and the compass pencil and fix in position (a screw is provided for this). Keep the compass point firmly in contact with the paper and slowly move the pencil arm around to form the circle. Alternatively, draw around a dinner plate to make a large circle, or around a jar lid or yogurt carton for medium-size circles, or around a bottle cap for small circles.

Odds and Ends Box

In preparation for craft activities, and so that you do not have to turn the house upside down every time your child gets the craft making urge, do encourage your child to collect handy things and provide him with a box for that purpose. Objects worth saving include: cardboard tubes, yogurt containers, bottle caps, jar lids, cereal boxes, matchboxes, thick cardboard, paper plates, lollipop sticks, candy wrappers, tissue paper, wrapping paper, color magazines, felt, string, fabric scraps, ribbons, cotton spools, corks, tinsel, pipe cleaners, sequins, glitter, straws, self-adhesive shapes, pinecones, dried flowers, buttons and beads.

Modeling Tools

A child-size rolling pin is advisable for rolling out play dough, salt dough and clay prior to cutting. For cutting, children can use a round-ended knife or modeling tool, bottle caps, jar lids and pastry cutters. Care should be taken with metal pastry cutters: if accidentally placed the wrong way up and pressed hard, they could cut the hand. Encourage children to create a variety of textures on the surface of dough and clay by experimenting with all sorts of household items from fork prongs to cotton spools. An old garlic press makes great clay 'hair.'

Modeling Materials

Play Dough is quick and simple to make, but as it does need cooking in a pan, adult assistance is required. The pan can be cleaned easily if it is put in to soak in warm soapy water right away.

Play dough can be stored in an airtight container in the refrigerator; when it is taken from the refrigerator it may require a few drops of oil to be kneaded into it to make it pliable.

Salt Dough can be baked in an oven, decorated and varnished, so that models made with it can be kept forever. In the recipe given on page 46 only a rough guide to the amount of water needed is provided. It is important to add the water a little at a time, until the salt dough leaves the bowl and hands clean. If the dough becomes slightly tacky, add a little flour and work it into the mixture. Salt dough is best made the day before it is required. Store in a plastic bag in the refrigerator. Before using, knead well on a lightly floured board.

When joining large areas of salt dough (and clay), lightly scratch the surface with a knife first. For smaller areas, lightly moisten with water and join two pieces together smoothing them carefully to hide the join.

Before baking modeled articles, brush lightly with a little water to give a good finish. Place items on a lightly greased baking sheet or on silicon-finished baking parchment. Salt dough should be cooked slowly in the oven on a low heat 250°F. Small articles will take about 1–2 hours; larger models will need 3–4 hours. Better still, cook overnight on the lowest setting. If possible turn the salt dough models over halfway through baking to ensure that they are cooked through.

NOTE: Salt dough cannot be cooked in a microwave oven.

Air-hardening Clay does not need a kiln to harden it; it will dry hard in a few days if left in a cool, dry place. It can be bought in 1lb or 2lb bags from art and craft stores. Once opened, the clay will keep if wrapped in foil or plastic wrap and placed in a plastic bag.

Papier-Mâché is a cheap and versatile modeling material made from old newspapers and a flour and water paste. There are two methods for making papier-mâché:

The Layered Method: Lay strips of torn newspaper over a mold and paste each layer with a flour paste made from approximately 2 heaped tablespoons all-purpose flour mixed with $1/3$ cup water.

The Pulp Method: Tear newspaper into small squares and mix with a flour paste made from approximately 2 heaped tablespoons all-purpose flour to $2/3$ cup water to make a malleable pulp. Making pulp papier-mâché is a messy business: use old but clean containers and wear rubber gloves.

Before decorating, papier-mâché models must be left for several days to dry out completely in a dry, moderately warm place, such as a pantry shelf, otherwise mold will form.

Modeling Plaster (plaster of Paris) can be purchased from most art and craft stores. It is normally mixed at 2 portions of plaster to 1 of water, but this may vary slightly. Plastic packaging from food products makes excellent molds. Wipe the mold with undiluted dishwashing liquid so that it will release the plaster cast easily once it has set. If the mold will not come away, it can be cut with scissors and carefully stripped. Be warned, modeling plaster sets quickly so do have your molds prepared before mixing it up.

USEFUL TIPS

• Always put a piece of tape over staples for safety.
• When gluing together two bits of cardboard, use a paper clip to hold them in place.
• Keep a template in place with a paper clip or a piece of tape.
• To make a neat hole in a piece of cardboard, lay the cardboard over a flattened ball of play dough and pierce with a sharp pencil or knitting needle.
• An awl is also useful for making neat holes through thick or decorated cardboard.
• When your child is cutting around a shape, she will find it easier to roughly trim off the excess paper or cardboard first before cutting neatly around the outline.

MAKING A TEMPLATE

To make a reusable cardboard template, lay a piece of tracing paper over the required template on pages 123–125. Draw around the outline with a pencil. Turn the tracing paper over and scribble over the pencil outline. Turn the tracing paper over once again and lay down onto a piece of thin cardboard. Carefully draw around the pencil outline. Remove the tracing paper. The outline of the traced shape on the cardboard may be quite faint. Go over it with black felt-tip pen. Cut out and label the cardboard template and keep it in a safe place. Use the cardboard template to draw around as many times as is needed onto paper, cardboard or fabric.

Published 1994 by Merehurst Limited
Ferry House, 51-57 Lacy Road, Putney,
London SW15 1PR

Reprinted in 1994

Project Editor: Cheryl Brown
Designer: Anita Ruddell
Photography by Jon Bouchier

Typeset by Litho Link Ltd, Welshpool, Powys, Wales
Color separation by Scantrans Pte Limited, Singapore
Printed in Italy by G. Canale & C., S.p.A.

Acknowledgments
The publisher would like to thank the staff and children of Riversdale Primary School, London Borough of Wandsworth, The Early Learning Centre, Phoebe Wood-Wheelhouse, Allie Johnstone, Lewis Elwin, Sharjeel Chaudary, Lee Richmond, Joseph Mills-Brown and Rand Hashim for their help in producing the photographs for this book.